Praise for *Power of Value Selling*

"Julie is a brilliant innovator, teacher, and leader in the most critical skill needed for success: How to sell with integrity. Julie's book ensures you are prepared to overdeliver for the customer despite the economic, technological, and environmental factors driving change. Its customer-centric approach puts the buyer at the core of every conversation. It guides the seller to proceed with the buyer to capture value, resulting in predictable, profitable growth. Having value selling as an integral part of your GTM initiatives is critical to your sales organization standing above your competitors. Generating scalable, profitable revenue takes a work. Make it easier by incorporating value selling in your sales process. It will be one of the best decisions you will ever make."

—Tim Marken
Managing Partner, Leonidas Strategy Group

"The magic for B2B companies happens when sellers align with buyers' actual needs to deliver real value and career-changing results. Julie teaches it in a way that is straightforward, arming readers with structure to apply in every customer conversation. The ValueSelling methodology distills the complexity of modern selling in a way that works for organizations of all sizes and across industries. Sellers benefit at any stage of their career. The ValueSelling framework up-levels every interaction to naturally accelerate better outcomes and deliver big results. A salesperson transforms into a trusted advisor, new customers are set up for success, and lifelong, high-value partnerships flourish. Whether you're looking to strengthen your sales skills or looking for a fresh perspective, this book is a fast-paced read with powerful insights and actionable takeaways that can change your work right away. I've seen many millionaires made and powerful businesses built by embracing ValueSelling."

—Michelle Allmond
Enterprise Sales Executive, Totango

"The fundamental lesson I teach to the students is when the value of the decision is greater than the risk, a sales person will have success. Value Selling teaches people how to find out what is important to an individual which then creates a map to create value. Once value confirmed with a prospect, the ability to win a sale is within reach. Julie's book, is an important and compelling read for anyone in the world of sales. With its practical strategies and real-world examples, it offers a comprehensive understanding of how to achieve greater success in selling products, themselves or great ideas."

—Follett Carter
Former EVP Sales & Marketing, Gartner Group Inc.
Director of the Sales Certificate Program
Stephen Ross School of Business, University of Michigan

"In today's landscape of selling, Sales and Enablement leaders need to transform their teams to the way that is focused on solutions, not products. Reps will have "a-ha" moments that you will see right before your eyes. The effectiveness of value selling clearly originates at the top, with Julie. Her guidance, depth of knowledge, and means of tactically executing programs is some of the best I have seen in my career."

—John Chinello
Senior Director, Sales Readiness, F5

"The concept is timeless, and it works. *The Power of Value Selling* delivers a fresh perspective on how modern buyers want to buy. It is a must-read if you're interested in sales training and coaching."

—Richard Eldh
Founder, Emeritus SiriusDecisions, Inc.

"I highly recommend the book for anyone looking to improve their sales skills. Julie has successfully separated ValueSelling from the rest. Whether you're a seasoned leader, seller, or just starting out, this book offers valuable insights that can help you become more effective and successful."

—Roderick Jefferson
Founding Member, Sales Enablement Society
CEO, Roderick Jefferson & Associates

"Julie Thomas shares valuable insights like, How we sell is just as important as what we sell, and How to negotiate on value not price. The ValueSelling methodology is designed to help you accelerate sales regardless of your product, service, or industry and regardless of how long you have been working in sales. *The Power of Value Selling* is an informative, fast-paced book for any salesperson looking to elevate their game, stand out from the crowd and be more successful."

—Kevin McHugh
Sales Capability Manger—APAC, Kimberly
Clark Professional

"What you will learn in Julie's book is the critical importance of how buyers want to buy as opposed to how sellers want to sell. The framework effectively addresses this gap. A wonderful and brilliant read for sales leaders who want to truly dominate their space!"

—Bradford Speaks
CEO, of BeLegendary.Coach

"I have come across numerous books claiming to hold the secret to sales success. However, none have resonated with me as deeply as *The Power of Value Selling* by Julie Thomas. Thomas expertly lays out a comprehensive framework that revolutionizes the way we approach sales. She understands that true success lies in creating enduring relationships with customers, built on trust, mutual respect, and long-term value creation. The book acts as a roadmap, guiding us through every step of the value-selling and buying journey.

Thomas' emphasis aligns perfectly with the modern sales landscape. Where customers are more informed than ever before, so traditional sales tactics fall short. "Value Selling" equips us with the tools and knowledge necessary to position ourselves as trusted advisors, providing tangible value and creating mutually beneficial partnerships.

This book is an invaluable resource for any sales professional in today's competitive market. Julie Thomas's expertise shines through, and her passion for empowering others is palpable. I wholeheartedly endorse this book and encourage anyone in sales watch their success soar."

—Todd Quarfot
Former CSO, Primepay
VP, Business Development & Strategic
Partnerships, Velocity Advisory Group

"Julie Thomas makes a compelling case that in today's market, customers are looking for more than just a product or service. They want a solution that delivers real value to their business. And as sales professionals, it is our job to demonstrate that to our customers. What I love about this book is how practical it is. From identifying customer pain points to crafting compelling value propositions, the book provides actionable advice that can be applied to any sales situation. You're a seasoned sales professional or just starting in the field, this book is packed with strategies that can help you succeed in today's competitive market. It truly is the gold standard for value selling."

—Corey White
Founder and CEO, Cyvatar

"I am a fan! As a 'bag carrying' sales manager, I am able to see the quantifiable business results ValueSelling has been able to achieve. The approach offers a framework and tools that are practical and effective. While some competitors may be in the business of selling workshops, *The Power of Value Selling* is focused behavioral change that results in sustained sales improvement."

—Joel Wecksell
Managing Partner, The Skills Connection

"Simple. Impactful. Relevant. Julie Thomas has created the definitive guide to building the business relationships that will result in predictable revenue growth. As more companies align their GTM motions around customer value, this practical playbook to sophisticated communication and human-to-human connection will become the standard for customer-obsessed companies."

—Melissa Widner
CEO, Lighter Capital

"*The Power of Value Selling* is an indispensable guidebook for sales professionals hoping to improve their results. With nearly half of buyers preferring an experience without reps, sales professionals need to adopt customer-centric practices if they hope to succeed. Julie Thomas provides a thorough roadmap for making sales-people trusted business advisors for buyers. Thomas provides practical advice and real-world examples that can assist sales professionals in today's complex B2B sales environment. I highly recommend this book to any reader interested in refining their selling approach and driving revenue growth."

—Dale Robinette
Coach and Consultant
Master Chair, Vistage Worldwide
Scaling Up Coach (Verne Harnish)

"Julie Thomas is a renowned expert and has helped countless companies achieve significant growth. *The Power of Value Selling* is a must read for all revenue professionals. Julie teaches sales teams how to build deep relationships with customers, understand their unique needs and challenges, and communicate the value of their products or services in a way that resonates with their prospects. Her innovative approach to sales training that yields results, with emphasis on customer success, and thought leadership make her a valuable asset to any organization looking to transform their sales approach and drive growth. I highly recommend you buy her book, and put the principles into practice, and see your revenue results increase dramatically!"

—Sandra Yancey
Founder and CEO, eWomenNetwork

THE POWER OF

THE GOLD STANDARD

VALUE

TO DRIVE REVENUE

SELLING

AND CREATE CUSTOMERS FOR LIFE

JULIE THOMAS

WILEY

Published by John Wiley & Sons, Inc., Hoboken, New Jersey.
Published simultaneously in Canada.

For general information on our other products and services or for technical support, please
contact our Customer Care Department within the United States at (800) 762-2974, outside
the United States at (317) 572-3993 or fax (317) 572-4002.

Wiley also publishes its books in a variety of electronic formats. Some content that appears in
print may not be available in electronic formats. For more information about Wiley products,
visit our web site at www.wiley.com.

Library of Congress Cataloging-in-Publication Data is Available:

ISBN: 9781394182565 (Cloth)
ISBN: 9781394182589 (ePub)
ISBN: 9781394182572 (ePDF)

Cover Design: Wiley
Cover Image: Courtesy of Lorin Yeater
Author Photo: © eWomenNetwork, Inc.

SKY10052224_072823

To the world-class ValueSelling Associates team and our clients.

Contents

Foreword—The Power of Value Selling: The Gold Standard to Drive Revenue and Create Customers for Life

The world of sales is changing, but not necessarily in the ways that you think.

Gartner recently reported, "In a survey of 725 B2B buyers . . . revealed that 72% of customers said they prefer a *rep-free experience*, or completing their purchase without speaking to a rep at any point."[1]

Does that surprise you? It probably shouldn't. If you have to speak with an agent while you're at the airport, it probably means you're having a bad day, right? When you order takeout and have to verbally order versus just doing it via app or online, that feels like work, right?

When you want to make a purchase for your business and find that you have to be "qualified" first and "discovered" second to even earn the right to speak with an "account executive," that's where the 72% as Gartner pointed out grows to 98%. The average salesperson is a nuisance. The average salesperson is annoying. The average selling process is off-putting. None of this should be considered news.

We've been hearing the four words "buyers know more nowadays" for over 100 years, followed by concerns regarding the future value of the sales professional.

Those four words, *"buyers know more nowadays,"* can first be found in Thomas Herbert Russell's 1912 book, *Salesmanship*.

It was a time when the rise of catalogs, mail order, and advertising was seen as a threat to the selling profession. I would be willing to bet that 72% of customers preferred a rep-free experience back then too!

As recently as 2015, "Forrester forecasts 1 million US B2B salespeople will lose their jobs to self-service eCommerce by 2020, accounting for 20% of the B2B sales force."[2]

In each case, the opposite happened. The profession grew, thrived, and continues to thrive—for those who see the threats and perceptions as an opportunity.

> "Today, people are educated to so many wants, the instruments of advertising are so universal, the sense of comparative buying is so keen that truth and value have made selling a profession."

This quote is from George S. Jones, Jr., who was the vice president of sales for a company called Servel, Inc. in 1947. It tells us all we need to know about why the future of sales and why what's written in the pages that follow presents an opportunity for you.

Let's re-read that ending together again. *"The sense of comparative buying is so keen that truth and value have made selling a profession."*

"Truth" and "Value."

As it turns out, the proliferation of information and feedback on everything we do, buy, and experience hasn't made it easier for buyers to buy; it's made it harder! Buyers have countless opportunities to improve their business processes and outcomes but can only focus on a small number at a time. Which ones do they choose?

We, as human beings, don't make purchasing decisions when we're *convinced*. Or if we do, we're typically not very happy about it. We make decisions when we can *predict*. We are prediction machines. We are seeking a prediction of whether this purchase is worth my limited inventory of time, resources, and dollars. Will the juice be worth the squeeze versus the other opportunities to improve the business and our lives?

Truth: People cannot predict if they don't trust the source of the information they are using to inform said prediction.

Value: People prioritize other opportunities when the ability to predict is difficult to achieve, where there's too much information available, and the onus of homework is all on the buyer. Consensus selling is hard. Consensus buying is harder!

The buyer's prediction begins with the first interaction. Is this individual here to help me, or to sell me? With every interaction, we are either building trust, or eroding trust . . . it's rarely staying the same.

The original design of the sales profession was as a service profession. As Arthur Sheldon proclaimed in his 1911 book, *The Art of Selling*, "True salesmanship is the science of service. Grasp that thought firmly and never let go."

The profession of sales will continue to flourish and, dare I say, rebuild its perception as a trusted and respected profession when we fully embrace the concepts of *truth* and *value*.

The ValueSelling Framework was the embodiment of those two words early in my leadership career, and continues to be today. Easy to understand and implement, it built confidence in my teams, allowing each individual to be a Sherpa to the buyer instead of a friction-building necessary evil. Having a structure built on a bed of trust, designed to illuminate the true mutual value, paint the journey, and help the buyer predict led to considerably larger deal sizes, faster selling cycles, better qualification in (and out), and created an extra differentiator— differentiating in the way we sold.

Embrace the pages that follow, and embrace the words of Arthur Dunn in 1919:

If the truth won't sell it, don't sell it.

Truth and value. ValueSelling.

Todd Caponi
Author and Speaker

Todd Caponi is the author of the three-time best-book-award-winning and international best-seller, *The Transparency Sale*, and the new best-selling book, *The Transparent Sales Leader*. Todd is a multi-time C-level sales leader, a behavioral science and sales history nerd, and has guided two companies to successful exits. He now speaks and teaches revenue organizations and their leaders on leveraging transparency and decision science to maximize their revenue capacity as Principal of Sales Melon LLC.

Introduction: The More Things Change, the More They Stay the Same

Selling value is more important today than it was even 16 years ago when I published my first book, *ValueSelling: Driving Sales Up One Conversation at a Time*. While quite a bit about selling is still as true today as it was in 2006, a significant transformation has also occurred.

Value is how people decide what to buy. It is the foundation for justifying the expenditure, the essence of how people answer the question, *Is it worth it?*

The most intriguing thing about value is that it's personal. Each of us makes buying decisions, based on our point of view and opinion of what is significant and relevant. Two people can make the same decision on what is valuable and have two completely different explanations regarding how they came to that conclusion.

Let's get this out of the way first: *Selling value is not the same as understanding your value proposition.* Of course, having a value proposition is important if your business is going to thrive. Your value proposition is your broad promise to the marketplace of where you can have a positive impact on their business. It's typically on a macro level: *We save you time and money.* Selling value is taking that generic promise and quantifying it for a specific organization and individual: *How much time we will save you. How much money we can save you. Do you, the buyer, believe and agree that savings is attainable?* With these pieces in place, a sales professional can then find out if that quantified savings *is enough* to motivate the prospect to change.

Understanding how your customer defines value is the foundation of this book—and value isn't merely about cost. As a buyer, I've been asked, *If this were free, would you implement it?* It's a thought-provoking question, and my answer is typically, *No*. Because even if a solution is free, it still requires me to spend *time* and *energy* to get it up and running with in-house management or an outside provider or change to a new paradigm to solve problems that were previously assumed to be unsolvable.

To sell change, you need to understand the why behind the buy and understand the customer's thought process.

■ ■ ■

For as long as there has been commerce, there have been buyers, and there have been sellers. Sales is a profession based on effective communication. Communication is more than presenting, pitching, or educating a prospect on what you do and why they should consider doing business with you. It's listening, making connections, storytelling, being relevant, and adding value to all the people involved in the process.

Since 2006, quite a bit has changed. Digital transformation was the foundation of that change. Another obvious change is the pandemic that hit in 2020, where virtually every sales professional around the globe had to redefine their approach and gain new skills. We lost the luxury of establishing relationships by being together and sharing experiences. Sales reps who depended on face-to-face meetings to build relationships and establish trust had to find a new way to achieve that objective. Sales executives who had always worked in a tech-enabled office with lots of colleagues, infrastructure, and community quickly had to adapt to a work-from-anywhere environment that did not afford the ease of collaboration and strategizing.

And it worked. We overcame it. We adapted. We pivoted, learned new skills, and used new technology. We became comfortable with our onscreen selves.

Buyers have also changed. How they buy has changed. What they expect has changed. It is imperative the sales rep change as well.

The prevalence of information available to buyers has impacted the way they buy and their expectations of sales professionals. No longer does the prospect have to meet with the seller to glean information about the products and services. The salesperson no longer controls the flow of information or even the source of information to the prospect. The prospect selects the sources and how and when they consume that information.

Complexity also has increased for buyers. The options and alternatives are vast, and it's difficult for the buyer to determine the nuanced value-add between various suppliers. If you don't believe me, look at your top competitors' websites and see if you can tell the difference between your offering and theirs. It's mind-boggling for buyers who have to navigate the conflicting— yet eerily similar—marketing messaging and approaches of the various vendors in any given space.

The number of people involved in most buying decisions has increased. With that increase, communication, collaboration, and consensus is more complex than with a single point of contact or decision-maker.

You can't overlook the role of technology—it has completely changed how sales reps prepare, execute, and follow up with individuals who are potential prospects for their products and services. Our buyers are bombarded with requests for demos and 10-minute meetings in the chance that maybe, *just maybe*, there might be a way to work together in the future. In some cases, the messaging from sales professionals is so bad that the communication actually hurts them as opposed to helping them.

Don't get me wrong: Technology absolutely has a role in sales. It allows you to automate mundane tasks. It allows you to accelerate tasks, amplify messaging, and enables you to analyze what is happening and shape future decision-making for the better. Technology also reduces the nonselling activities sales professionals have hated, complained about, or just flat refused for years. It's foolish to argue against the advancements in efficiency that sales tech provides—but efficiency alone won't change our results. We need to be effective.

There is one thing that sales tech cannot do: It cannot replace the magic that happens when a human connection is made.

Let's face it: If sales technology could solve the sales productivity problem that many organizations face today, that problem would have been solved a long time ago.

■ ■ ■

I've written *The Power of Value Selling: The Gold Standard for Driving Revenue and Creating Customers for Life* to explore one simple fact: the idea that how we sell is just as important as what we sell.

This book is based on practical experience and application we've gleaned by working with hundreds of thousands of sales professionals in thousands of organizations around the globe to improve the efficacy of their selling motion.

There is no question that organizations that deploy a consistent selling motion across their entire revenue organization outperform those that don't. This book will give you a behind-the-scenes glimpse into the best practices that leading sales organizations around the world adopt to ensure their sales professionals are as effective as humanly possible.

Leading ValueSelling Associates for the past 20 years has taught me a number of lessons. One of the most profound is that change is hard. While many may *want change*, they don't want to *be changed*. However, we must change to survive. One of the key traits of any sales professional today is adaptability and agility.

This book isn't merely for account executives and sales leaders—everyone sells. Yes, everyone! If you speak with prospects or customers, you are a part of the revenue team or sales, whether it is in your title or not—the customer doesn't care about your title. When speaking with anyone, there is an opportunity to either contribute to or contaminate the perception of your company.

If you are part of the revenue engine for your company or want to be, this book is for you. The tactics and processes described in this book are for all business-to-business (B2B) professionals. B2B is not limited just to commercial enterprises. If you sell to any organization, you are a B2B sales professional. That includes, for example, government, health care, not-for-profit organizations, professional organizations, and education.

This book covers the entire life cycle of a revenue team, from creating prospects out of suspects to developing and qualifying opportunities to closing and delivering measurable outcomes—I'll also walk you all the way through upsell and renewals. Yes, I'll address the process in stages, but you have to remember that this is not a linear process. It's a circular and iterative cycle that creates a complicated puzzle that you need a framework for managing.

I've divided this book into five sections. In the first part, we'll dive into what's changed and how our discipline has adapted. Part II will address what you, the sales professional, must do in this fast-paced world. In Part III, we'll look at filling the revenue funnel and creating winnable opportunities, and Part IV will cover how to advance and close these opportunities in this new environment. Finally, in Part V, I'll disclose all the secrets you'll need to create raving fans who are customers for life.

If your objective is to be a world-class sales professional or to lead a sales organization of world-class sellers, this is the only guide you'll need. It's pragmatic and focused on actionable best practices that generate immediate and sustainable sales results.

– Julie Thomas

Why ValueSelling, Why Now

1

Specialized Sellers, Exploding Sales Tech, Sophisticated Buyers (What's Changed)

Within 7 minutes of meeting Natalie, you say more than you intended. Don't get me wrong—you haven't caught yourself reciting your Social Security number or disclosing a long-hidden phobia; you have discussed a personal or business piece of information that you would not normally tell most new business acquaintances. Don't worry; Natalie isn't a grifter. She's a sales professional specializing in enterprise-level SaaS sales.

Natalie is one of these magnetic people you immediately connect with, one who seems to unconsciously solicit crucial information from simple, well-timed questions, listens with intent, and effortlessly gets to the heart of the matter. She's also becoming obsolete.

According to Gartner, sales will see the death of data entry and the rise of synthetically generated sales outreach and machine customers—all within the next 5 years.[1]

What does this mean?

It means it's not difficult to picture a future where the most time-consuming tasks of a seller's day become automated: Data capture is instantaneous; sales cadences and content are optimized using digital representations of prospects; buyers use automated procurement processes.

Now, what happens if we take this one step further?

It's not hard to imagine a future where personal and professional data are compiled to create and feed alarmingly accurate digital twins of business-to-business (B2B) buyers. In this reality, outreach and marketing campaigns are tested against a sophisticated data warehouse containing every interaction from prospects and buyers who fit the same customer profile. Then, assuming some manual intervention is needed, the salesperson merely follows the AI-prescribed actions and scripts to the deal's conclusion.

Yes, this is creepy—to say the least. And a slew of privacy and ethical considerations need to be confronted along the way. However, it's not out of the question that the sales world of the 2030s will resemble this hypothetical reality.

You have to ask yourself: *Is the long-prophesized death of the salesperson imminent?*

■ ■ ■

Let's step back and look at how we got here. To fully understand the modern B2B buyer—and why most would rather watch paint dry than engage with your outreach cadences—we have to first understand the underlying mechanisms that introduce friction into the buying process.

Specialized Sellers When I first started out in sales, there were two roles: hunter/farmer or finder/minder. Most of us cold-called, identified opportunities, worked those opportunities until we won or lost, and we were responsible for handling the renewal. Although, the system worked—it was also horribly inefficient.

This revelation ushered in an era of specialization with hyper-focused selling roles: sales development representatives (SDRs) for creating new opportunities, account executives (AEs) for converting those opportunities into new business and logos, sales engineers for showing the capabilities of your solution, and customer success and post-sales engineers for managing the implementation and ensuring customers received the expected value. And that is just the beginning.

It's a tremendous system, on paper.

The reality tends to play out differently. You're talking about hundreds of touchpoints across the life cycle of a single contract. And to maintain a consistent customer experience, each of those touchpoints must contain all of the relevant customer information for a given action. If you ever played the game "telephone" in elementary school, you know salient points get lost whenever information is transferred, and the more transfers you have, the bigger the distortion. This is the best-case scenario.

The problem becomes more complicated when you add in the tremendous churn we've seen in recent years. Even before the Great Reshuffle, it wasn't uncommon for XaaS clients to have three or four account managers over the course of a year. In the case where all sales roles assigned to an account stay at a company, there's still the issue of people moving up and down the org chart, which happens more rapidly than you might think at large companies. And if you're dealing with a rapidly growing company, you also have to consider the impact of reassigning coverage models—swapping personnel and account structures to accommodate acquisitions and new hires.

The result is the need for frequent re-education of sales professionals. By whom? Well, if you don't educate yourself or your company doesn't educate you, the only party left is your customer. They have absolutely no interest in doing so.

Keep in mind that we're still talking about the best-case scenario here: Everyone has performed the correct action at the correct time. Of course, this is never the case, but it works to illustrate the scale of the strain that the most well-run sales organizations are compelled to put on customer relationships.

Exploding Sales Tech   You're probably already familiar with the infamous MarTech Map that shows a whopping 9,932 solutions for 2022.

Let that sink in. Nine thousand, nine hundred, thirty-two solutions. If you look up the zoomed-out table, it's all but unintelligible—the symbols on display resemble a convoluted and color-coded version of Morse code. The sales tech side of things is shaping up to follow suit: Nancy Nardin of Smart Selling Tools compiled a graphic for the 2022 marketplace that features more than 1,000 solutions, and the Salesforce app exchange lists more than 7,000 applications.

And this exploding market doesn't plan on slowing down anytime soon. According to Gartner, 93.6% of sales leaders are investing in sales tech, and by 2025, 92% of large enterprises worldwide will be using sales tech in their daily workflows.[2]

Now, I want to make one thing clear: Sales tech can be a tremendous tool for sellers to leverage. It helps you automate, amplify, and execute efficiently at scale. Question any sales rep about their customer relationship management (CRM) hygiene, and you'll likely hear this in response: *Did you hire me to do data entry or talk to prospects?* And they're absolutely right.

In contrast, you run into problems when you start chasing efficiency and trusting in the fallacy that activity reliably correlates to success. I see it all the time: Sales leaders end up measuring the wrong leading indicators and encouraging the volume of activities, not the quality of the behaviors. Let me show you what I mean.

In July 2022, I took a call with a frustrated chief executive officer (CEO). It was a small tech company that had recently taken on private equity and needed to paint a picture of sales activity for investors. They'd had some initial success, so they dove into the data and began extrapolating: *If 100 emails translate to five meetings, then 500 emails will translate to 25 meetings, and 1,000 emails will…*

You see where this is going.

Immediately following this revelation, the mandate came down that every seller needed to send 1,100 emails and add 225 contacts to Salesforce *each day*. They rolled this out at their SKO in January 2022, and by the end of June, they'd sent roughly 256,000 emails to prospects.

How many new opportunities were generated as a result?

You guessed it—zero.

While this situation may sound incredible, it happens all the time. Sales leaders fail to interrogate *the why* behind wins, and they set goals for a volume of activity that eliminate the possibility of careful, methodical action. Or, they fall into the trap of assuming that scaling success is merely a tech problem.

■ ■ ■

What's the end product of all this *efficiency?*

These five negative effects are the most common:

1. Hurts the brand: Wrongly targeted outreach damages your company's brand reputation. A survey by Lusha shows that 80% of buyers indicate they are put off when receiving irrelevant information from companies looking to sell to them, and 29% say they're unlikely to do business with the company as a result.[3]

2. Loss of sales: Poorly targeted outreach can result in an ongoing (52%) and/or immediate (37%) loss of sales, according to the same study.

3. Builds bad habits: Sales tech often leads to reps relying on untargeted techniques rather than using tech and data to make sales the ultra-focused and personalized process it should be.

4. Treats prospects like commodities, not people: Sending emails that are only about your product and your need to book a meeting are a waste of time. It tells the prospect that you didn't do your research to understand how you can add value to them.

5. Damages sales team morale: When sellers focus the majority of their time and energies on activities that lead to, at best, sporadic results, they feel more like cogs in a machine than strategic professionals. As a result, morale plummets. Many sales representatives report that all this efficiency and technology is actually a barrier to productivity.

How do sophisticated B2B buyers feel about having their inboxes and voicemails flooded with nonrelevant sales pitches and irrelevant messages?

Suffice it to say that buyer backlash is growing—there's a reckoning on the horizon.

Sophisticated Buyers

Make no mistake—today's B2B buyer is in the driver's seat, so much so that salespeople are lucky to be riding in the same metaphorical car. Buyers are knowledgeable, sophisticated, and have zero tolerance for vendors and suppliers who are unprepared. They set the ground rules for communication and how and when they want to buy. Let's face it: They're impatient because they think they know it all—and sometimes they're right. They are also impatient because many sales professionals have not listened, added value, or made relevant connections with the buyer.

Today's buyers are more educated than ever before, and how they become educated has evolved. Long gone are the days when the messaging about your products and services was controlled by your company's marketing or sales teams. Every customer, employee (current and former), supplier, and partner now has a megaphone to share any perspective or opinion about your company—and there is no filter or safeguard on how this shapes a buyer's perspective. In fact, peer networks and reviews often hold more weight or value than your company's official information and product education efforts.

As a result, buyers are comfortable with digital research and buying, expect part of the process to be online or hybrid, and expect to dictate the proper mix of online and offline communication according to their preferences. In short, buyers are far less dependent on salespeople, and it's a trend that I expect to continue.

This means that sales professionals are becoming involved in the purchasing process much later than in the past—sometimes, we are being eliminated from the process completely. If and when we are brought in, it's closer to the end of the buying journey to discuss pricing and packaging and not necessarily to educate or inform the buyer.

This would be enough to chew on by itself, but you cannot understate the rapid changes since the onset of the COVID-19 pandemic. Looking back at the first 2 years of the pandemic, B2B sales saw more than a few headlines that turn heads:

- Seventy-two percent of B2B customers prefer a rep-free experience.[4]
- "Often, B2B buyers don't buy the best solution but rather choose the lowest-risk solution."[5]
- "While Gen Xers generally have larger budgets than millennials, the 'heads down' generation now dominates B2B purchase decisions."[6]

If that's not enough to make your head spin, look at the 2022 survey by Bain and Google. It revealed that most tech salespeople hold serious misconceptions about buyer behavior:

> Fully 80%–90% of respondents, depending on what they are buying, have a set of vendors in mind before they do any research. Just as important, 90% of them will ultimately choose a vendor from the initial list.[7]

This fits with my experience. Increasingly, buyers are narrowing their field of possible sources through the use of requests for information (RFI) and requests for proposals (RFP). Today's purchasing process is often designed to minimize the amount of information provided to the salesperson and focuses the entire discussion on capabilities, deliverables, and price. This puts you at a disadvantage in understanding the context of the purchase and the perspectives of all the stakeholders involved. Most impactfully, it limits your ability to uncover personal motivations and create collaborative solutions or alternatives.

When you zoom out and look at the buying group, you'll find further shifts. Gartner reports that the average buying group for complex purchases is made up of 6–10 individuals who only spend 17% of their time meeting with potential vendors or suppliers.[8] I'm here to tell you that's the low end of things. It's not uncommon for B2B buying groups at the enterprise level to reach well into the mid-20s.

For example, in 2021, I was invited to present to a team of global managers involved in a procurement decision. My company was a finalist, and this was part of the beauty contest to compare the vendors. I thought 25 people was huge. However, almost 40 ended up in the Zoom meeting, and the call was recorded for the individuals who could not attend.

The makeup of these groups is also shifting. Power is much more distributed than before, and who has that power is in flux. For example, procurement was typically brought in at the end of the buying process; their job was to execute the decision made by someone else. Since 2021, they have a seat at that table from the start; they are now influencing the decision to a greater extent. No longer are they the final barrier in a negotiation, but a presence to define the requirements and help identify the shortlist. In fact, that same survey by Bain and Google also revealed the tendency of salespeople to only focus on high-level decision-makers, to their detriment.

What does all of this change mean for sales professionals?

Tremendous opportunity—if you play your cards right.

■ ■ ■

In 2021, my company partnered with Selling Power to survey 154 high-level sales leaders to examine what sets high-performing salespeople consistently apart from the rest of the pack.

What's the biggest difference we uncovered? The punchline is short and simple: their ability to be human.

All the tech in the world can't make a buyer trust you—and that's the crucial ingredient for large, complex purchases that have the power to seriously affect a buyer's career, especially in a world dominated by similar digital experiences, virtual selling, and commoditized markets.

Personally, I've seen this play out time and time again. High-performing reps routinely focus on the other person, their challenges, motivations, and goals. Yes, they read industry journals, financial reports, and the latest LinkedIn post from analyst firms; they listen to the shareholder calls and attend industry-specific webinars—they digest any information that will help them better understand the critical issues facing the company they're targeting.

Then they make it personal: *What set of key performance indicators (KPIs) is a potential buyer trying to meet or achieve? Would success result in industry recognition? Would failure mean they're suddenly out of a job? Is this decision career limiting or career defining?*

By adopting this mindset, they elevate the conversation above the transactional to connect on a human level that's authentic and demonstrates their desire to put the buyer first.

Ultimately, empathy is the foundational skill that makes all of the above effective. People will always be the most important aspect of any complex sales process—and when they're able to authentically connect at a human level, a strong business relationship is forged. It's those relationships that get deals done.

■ ■ ■

What does this mean for Natalie, our old friend from the beginning of the chapter?

Suddenly she's not looking so obsolete after all. She's looking more and more like that vital component to any company's success: a trusted business partner who can offer a convincing path to value realization tied to meaningful financial metrics. She is an empathetic seller who always puts the prospect's needs above her desire to close a sale. And she provides the one thing that AI can perhaps never give: *confidence*.

2

How You Sell Is Just as Important as What You Sell

Having spent more than 25 years in sales leadership, I've learned one certainty: *Change is inevitable—and the speed of change is accelerating.*

Buyers will make a purchase decision for a number of reasons. They could be on the hunt for a brand-new buy for a novel solution that has been identified to support a crucial initiative; they might be looking to rebuy a solution and are exploring options with multiple vendors; or perhaps they're replacing one solution with something completely different based on a new paradigm of how to address an existing need.

In the end, it doesn't matter. Regardless of the type of buy, how buyers buy has changed. That means how salespeople sell must also evolve.

■ ■ ■

Before we can evolve, we need to examine our understanding of what "sales" is at its core and the salesperson's role in the process.

From the beginning of commerce, selling has been defined as the transference of confidence. It flows from the seller to the buyer and is focused on solving problems that are *worth solving* in the buyer's mind. The salesperson's job is to facilitate the prospect's buying process, not to force the buyer to conform to the salesperson's methodology—and to do this you have to focus on the uniqueness of the buyer.

Every buyer's decision-making process is individual to that person and organization. Top-performing sellers not only acknowledge that individuality, they work with it, not against it. This includes an empathetic understanding of the immense pressure buyers face. It's no secret that buyers are risk-averse, and it's a trend that's become much more amplified in recent years. Throw in any economic uncertainty, and risk-aversion reaches a fever pitch. Buyers and executives are simply not willing to assume any risk in the purchasing process, and they expect an explicit return on their investment. Tasked with making the perfect business decision with imperfect information, it's only natural that B2B buyers seek to avoid making bad decisions that could be career-limiting or jeopardize the reputation of individuals involved in that decision.

You also have to consider how crowded and fragmented markets have become. The number of options facing prospects is vast. It's a maze of traditional vendors, niche players, and offshore alternatives that's difficult to navigate in two primary ways:

1. Because these options are so varied, it's challenging for buyers to determine how these differences will play out post-implementation and understand the unique value which may result from one alternative versus another.

2. Most companies' digital experiences and collateral are eerily similar to their competition, which requires more effort on the buyer's part to avoid conflating one product/solution with another.

And it's not merely one buyer. As I'll touch on more in the next chapter, you're dealing with expanding buying committees full of unique individuals who all have different needs, competing agendas, and preferred methods of interacting with content and salespeople. The complexity of the situation tends to grow exponentially with the size of the committee—imagine how the spider web of communication transforms when five buyers turn into 25!

Generational difference in communication preferences is a new wild card to consider. Many B2B salespeople who sell to enterprise accounts became familiar with selling to Gen Xers—except now, B2B purchasing is dominated by millennials.[1] Plus, the explosion of hybrid workforces has pushed communication and collaboration to evolve faster in the last 3 years than it has in the last 2 decades: Text, collaborative platforms, and customer portals have replaced email and other traditional modes of communication.

Long gone are the days when the salesperson was the only source of information about products and services—which only makes sense since not all sales reps were transparent in the capabilities they could bring to a prospective buyer. In turn, this led to the rise of peer insight forums and peer-review sites that buyers viewed as far more credible than the salespeople who were bombarding them with outreach and forcing them to match their agenda.

For example, my company was looking for a new sales engagement tool last year to help bolster our team's productivity. I did what any buyer would do: I identified the gap, did some research on leading suppliers, and developed a short list of vendors I wanted to speak with. Next, I took that list to my network and narrowed it down a little more based on their past experiences before handing the project off to a direct report who was tasked with identifying the ideal fit.

So far, so good, right?

Then came the actual outreach to vendors.

The first vendor she contacted never responded to an online request to speak with a salesperson. The second scheduled a short meeting to "qualify" the opportunity before assigning it to a sales rep, but their qualification process only included two questions: *What's your budget?* and *When do you want to buy?* The third simply shot over a link to an ebook and options to buy online.

I was shocked none of those vendors actually added value when we invited them into the conversation. Obviously, the vendor that chose not to respond was dismissed immediately. The other two were still in the race and chose to communicate the way *they wanted to communicate*, not the way we wanted to buy.

It wasn't pleasant.

The moral of the story is you must, must, must understand how buyers buy. Buyers expect information and insight when they want it, how they want it, and where they want it. You cannot dictate or control the communication—you must have the courage to turn over control to the buyer and add value to earn their trust.

■ ■ ■

If the buyer has changed so drastically, why hasn't the salesperson?

The answer is that salespeople who are and will continue to be successful *have* changed. They have proactively evolved their skills to manage this new world in which they operate. By leveraging technology, becoming more consultative and collaborative, and developing stronger communication skills, they've laid the foundations to be successful in today's marketplace, but that's merely table stakes.

Smart salespeople are purposeful in their preparation and execution—they understand and apply best practices consistently, and they repeat the formula for success again and again. They leave nothing to chance, don't wing it, and understand how outdated and foolish pitching is—instead, they engage. They build powerful, sustainable, personal relationships with their clients and prospects based on value-added interactions. Above all, they don't waste prospects' time.

Whenever I think about the magic of human-to-human connection in sales, I'm reminded of a story I want to share. Four years ago, I was at the funeral of a good friend, Dan. He'd been in sales for the majority of his career and had built a nice business working for a leading insurance provider in the United States. I'll never forget how powerful the company CEO's eulogy was: He said that what made Dan so effective was that he never tried to turn his friends into clients. Instead, he turned every client into a friend.

That's how you create customers for life.

How do you get a prospect to connect with the value you're offering, to the extent that it motivates them to choose your solution over someone else's? Yes, strong presentations and well-developed negotiation skills will help, but simply putting on a good show and talking circles around the competition isn't enough to be successful today. To generate immediate sales results and win customers for life, begin with a very basic and often overlooked concept: *Ask, don't tell.*

Product-led sales is falling by the wayside. It's not about you or your product. It's about the prospect—how you relate to them, uncover their wants and needs, and build a collaborative relationship to solve problems worth solving.

Salespeople today are as much consensus builders as representatives of the products and services they sell. Building the interpersonal skills to communicate effectively and efficiently with all the individuals involved in the purchase process is imperative. Agility is key. Good communicators understand that what they say and do is only half of what is required. At the end of the day, it doesn't matter what we say; what matters is what the prospect hears and understands. You'll also need to lean on these communication skills to resolve conflict because if there's one thing I know, it's this: The larger the purchase, the more people are involved, who all have competing views on what the right solution is, and thus the greater the potential for heated disagreement.

With these cross-functional buying committees, sales reps have to gain more insight into the various roles that they need to communicate with, listen to, and, ultimately, influence to ensure a positive outcome and sales result. In some cases, that requires the selling organization to create teams that match the buying organization.

Let's look at how that typically plays out.

If you have a technical buyer who is extremely knowledgeable and detailed in her need for information, you'll have to match that individual up with someone who can speak her language. Conversely, if you have an executive decision-maker who doesn't care at all about the technical specifications of your product, but is highly interested in the business outcomes that product will deliver, you'll need to bring in someone who is equipped to talk about the business outcomes your product will deliver. If your company handles the product but not the implementation, you may also need to bring in individuals from your partner ecosystem who will provide the roadmap for getting the buyer up and running.

Sales engineers, customer success, executive sponsors, and leaders are involved earlier and earlier in the sales process. It's not uncommon for account executives to take on the role of team captain—working to communicate with external audiences while collaborating internally to ensure the whole selling team and partner ecosystem has knowledge and clear direction, and understands their role in the process. The sales rep is now the crucial guide who facilitates the buying process—helping buyers navigate the maze of fragmented information and instilling confidence in their decisions.

Sales is the lifeblood of any business. It is the sales organization that manufactures revenue by converting prospects to paying customers.

Make no mistake. You, the salesperson have the ability to become one of your company's great assets—how you engage and add value can become your greatest differentiator.

You might have a clearly superior product, and if the buyer doesn't have a positive experience, you'll lose the sale anyway. Customer experience is the critical factor, and the customer demands a frictionless buying experience. If you want to be selected by the buyer, remember that how you sell—with an aim to engage, build trust, rapport, and consensus—is just as important as what you sell.

3

Modern Selling Is ValueSelling (Why Value Is Still Important)

Value is the only thing that matters to the buyer—or is it?

From a sales perspective, it's easy to argue that value-based selling is more important than ever. At the time of writing, anxiety about the economy has persisted for nearly 3 years, and as a result, the importance of justifying any purchase and building the required business case feels at an all-time high. Ask any sales leader, and they'll tell you that world-class sales organizations understand that equipping their revenue teams with a best practice approach, skillset, competencies, and toolset is no longer a luxury—it is imperative.

Where does the disconnect with buyers come from, then? On the surface, you'd think everyone would agree that value is paramount. There are two problems that stand in your way: lack of confidence and complexity.

Historically, we have expected sales professionals to know their products and industries. The premise is that if you can get a meeting, you can pitch your product or service to your prospect.

Many presentations had a very formulaic approach with a few common elements—here is the outline:

- Let me tell you about our founder—she is amazing!
- Let me show you a photo of our building—it is amazing!
- Let me show you the "NASCAR" logo slide of all the world-class companies that have already made the decision to be our customers—they are amazing!
- Let me tell you about my products—they are beyond amazing!
- Blah, blah, blah.

If value is what really matters, then why isn't that part of this formula?

I have learned that many executives in similar roles have the same challenges, and this holds true across different geographies and industries. Yet almost every time I speak with someone new, at some point in the conversation, I am told: *This is unique to us* or *You have probably never heard this before.*

That last point is critical. Buyers want to be heard. They want to be validated. They want to be understood and viewed as unique.

The sales rep has to acknowledge this fact. They have to work to personalize their messages and understand the context that creates the buyer's reality.

The heart of modern selling is buyer-centric. It is collaborative. It is not gimmicky. It builds trust through engagement.

Buyers will not be interested in you until you demonstrate interest in them.

Lack of Confidence   On the morning of April 2, 2022, a friend of mine woke to a strange headache and a sore throat. He did what anyone with an internet connection would do: started Googling symptoms.

After a negative COVID-19 test and 40 minutes of frantic searching, he'd decided on two scenarios, one probable, the other extremely unlikely:

1. He had a common cold. He needed more fluids, rest, and the occasional Advil. Worst case scenario, it would take a week for him to return to normal.
   - OR -
2. He'd come down with a rare and rapidly metastasizing type of brain cancer. In his mind, the connection was clear—after all, two of his symptoms were a perfect match. He needed an invasive, lengthy, and costly course of treatment that should have been started weeks ago. Best case scenario, all but certain death.

Was he confident in his diagnosis? No, of course not, but he genuinely believed both to be a possibility in the moment—and guess what?

This is exactly the boat modern buyers find themselves in.

Buyers don't know how to buy. They don't do it that often. They don't know what they don't know, and the last thing they want is to be sold. They don't know how to diagnose their problems, and therefore their prescriptive solution is off the mark.

They want to be heard, understood, and educated with value-added insight. They want the sales professional to guide them and add value throughout their buying process. And, in spite of that, they often jump to the wrong conclusions.

When people talk about inflation, they're typically referencing the economy; we're dealing with an inflation of information as well. There's too much information coming from too many sources and too little time to sort through it all. We're searching for solutions that underscore simplicity but are being bombarded with bits of information—everything is a sound bite and it's incredibly difficult to assess and understand that information on the fly. This leaves us with a fragmented understanding of what we think we need.

It can be overwhelming. It can be confusing. And when confused, most people will do *nothing*.

Yes, a buyer's power and desire to do self-directed research is immense, and it can be hard for them to understand the nuances between alternatives.

There's an exercise our facilitators run during some of our workshops that never fails to shock participants. In it, the facilitator presents the workshop participants with several pages of marketing copy, a mix of their company's materials and the competition's, scrubbed of all logos and identifying information such as product names. Nine times out of ten, salespeople can't even tell the difference. If these are individuals who are deeply familiar with their own products, you can only imagine how bewildering the buyer's experience must be. Brent Adamson touched on this point in his keynote for the 2021 Gartner CSO and Sales Leader Conference, revealing that 64% of B2B buyers cannot differentiate one brand's digital experience from another's.[1] Yikes!

The nature of modern work only complicates the issue further. All of us fall prey to the vortex of Slack notifications, emails, texts, scheduled meetings, impromptu calls and Zoom meetings, instructing direct reports, and generally bouncing between one task and another. And while all of this seems hectic enough, there's a hidden pitfall here that many don't fully understand.

Cal Newport wrote about it in *Deep Work: Rules for Focused Success in a Distracted World*. His research showed that when professionals switch between tasks, something called "attention residue" is created—you may think you've wholly moved on to that next task, but your brain is still somewhat focused on the previous task for up to 20 minutes after the fact.[2]

Now, play that out across the possibly hundreds of tasks that a B2B buyer navigates daily—it's a wonder business gets done at all. If only they had a trusted advisor to help them focus on the problems worth solving and make sense of all of the available information.

Enter the sales professional.

High-performing sellers have learned to show up as a trusted advisor there to solve a buyer's most critical business problems—and we have our work cut out for us. In addition to information overload and a fragmented work experience, salespeople are also facing serious trust issues. And with good reason.

In Forrester's 2021 B2B Trust Survey, they asked buyers to quantify the risk/reward of a recent purchase to both themselves and their organizations. Want to guess who they thought shouldered the majority of the risk? That's right, the buyer.[2] This explains why buyers are opting for the solution they perceive as the lowest risk over the ideal one. Plus, let's face it: Most B2B buyers have been burned in the past, especially when it comes to tech purchases. Skepticism runs deep, and buyers consciously and unconsciously set up barriers to establishing relationships with suppliers.

There's also the most overlooked part of the equation to consider: *change.*

No matter what you're selling, you're selling change. Never underestimate the power of the status quo. You might have the best solution in the marketplace, the only solution, even—but the prospect always has another choice. The choice to do nothing.

Complexity It is not that the sales process is complex. It is not. The buying process is complex.

Buying is a consensus decision right now; it involves a lot of people. The salesperson is essentially the ambassador who speaks the language of the host country and interprets the languages between all those stakeholders to make sure everyone understands the language of the buyers, and that they understand one another.

Complexity is a function of the number of people, agendas, preferences, and biases that come into a group decision.

People describe things differently based on where they sit in the organization—even if they are talking about the same thing; this kind of translation is essential. It only makes sense: The more people involved in a process, the more complex it becomes. The Forrester 2021 B2B Buying Study shows that the average number of buying interactions (both digital and in-person) from 2019 to 2021 grew from 17 to 27.[3] While each of those touchpoints may be shorter (a quick phone call or email versus an in-person demo or presentation), there are many more of them.

Here again, you can see the opportunity for information overload, especially when salespeople are feeding different information to different buyers as they navigate their own unique buying process asynchronously. More opportunities to receive information means more information to sort through and synthesize—and possibly more confusion. The same report also found that about 80% of B2B purchases involve these more-fragmented buying scenarios. It is essential for a sales rep to communicate with an operations person, a tech lead, and all the different roles on the buying committee—and build human-to-human connections with each person to uncover what they value.

At the end of the day, value is not a single-dimensional object—especially in a complex, enterprise sale with a large buying group and many different personal and professional filters.

Value Is NOT Just ROI   Early in my career, when I was still at Gartner, the company made a large software purchase. Now, this was before the jump to SaaS (software as a service), so you bought the software, then you cleared out a floor of your office building to house all the technicians and consultants who would help you implement. Not 2 years later, SaaS was exploding on the scene thanks to companies like Salesforce with scalable models that were comparably low-cost and so easy to implement you simply switched them on. Comparing the two examples, you immediately see the power of the SaaS value proposition. And that was enough for SaaS to win, until it wasn't.

Today, a company's value proposition is never powerful enough to justify the purchase on its own. In today's marketplace, ROI (return on investment) or COI (cost of inaction) is not always sufficient. When sales orgs conduct win/loss analyses for why the deals are lost or stalled, it's nearly always because the solution was not mapped to business issues and outcomes. You can have the best product/solution in the marketplace, successfully position yourself against competitive alternatives, prove the ROI of your solution, and still lose to no decision. To avoid this trap, sales professionals must fully understand and embrace the fact that true value and impact are uncovered when you focus on the problems worth solving—so how do you uncover them?

To uncover these business issues, salespeople must move beyond pain points and value propositions. Step one is to put on your physician's cap and properly diagnose the problem.

Looking back to my friend's somewhat humorous Google triage example, let's consider what would have happened if he'd gone so far as to call his doctor and demand treatment for his sudden, life-threatening illness.

What if she'd agreed?

Imagine: Instead of assuring him that he was jumping to conclusions and offering an appointment, she answers the phone and says, "Headache, sore throat. Yeah, there's no need to come in. I'll refer you to the oncologist and you should get your affairs in order."

What would he have done? Very politely hung up and started the search for a new doctor.

Admittedly, this thought experiment is somewhat far-fetched—but is it that far off from what salespeople do when they try to sell a product/service to a prospect before understanding the potential buyer's key business drivers and the problems that stand in their way?

The simple truth is that most sellers and buyers identify a challenge and only look at it from their perspective. This focuses their attention on the symptom and severely limits their ability to diagnose the underlying problems or root cause. It's only when you understand all of the underlying problems impacting a key business driver that you can begin to craft a solution that delivers true organizational value and differentiates you in a sea of sameness.

It may also be the classic case of *they don't know what they don't know*. To gain ground on the competition, growing companies quickly expand into new markets, with new products for new buyers. New ways of doing business are always full of new challenges, and given the novelty of the situation, B2B buyers might not know how to solve these problems, which is why sellers must ensure they gather as much information as possible before recommending any solution.

Salespeople often overlook this point and make the mistake of viewing discovery as a one-time event. As a result, it takes on a transactional light: *Give me this info, then I'll give you what you really want.* Sellers start the call and attempt to run through their list of questions. Typically, these are situational questions that are stacked at the beginning. This ends with the potential buyer feeling like they're being interrogated and putting their guard up. In contrast, high performers know that when you trade this transactional mindset for consultative business conversations, you better serve your potential buyers. You also radically improve your chances of uncovering business challenges that your product or service is uniquely qualified to solve. In doing so, you'll forge trusted business relationships and uncover the value that motivates individuals to act with urgency.

Urgency is a powerful ally when it comes to winning the fight for capital at the CFO (chief financial officer) level. Remember, ROI isn't enough—the sales cycle has bifurcated, and any large-scale purchase will have to win out against competing solutions. This is where the concept of personal value comes in.

Say it with me: *People make logical, business decisions for emotional, personal reasons.*

As a sales professional, your ultimate goal is to uncover what gets the executive decision-maker's heart beating faster and align with that, and it won't be easy. Procurement wants to block this motion. If they had it their way, buying would be a clinical and exacting science without all the mess that comes with human emotions. Thankfully, that will never happen, provided you can get a foot in the door and have these vital conversations with a C-suite executive.

For example, 12 years ago I was working a deal with one of my top performers. We were selling to an industry-leading CRM company. We'd established relationships with the executive decision-makers, built consensus on the problems worth solving, and created a roadmap for doing it. In short, things were looking good—until another vendor changed the rules of the game.

At the end of the buying process, after we'd already been told that we had won, procurement made a grand entrance and decided they need bids from our competitors—so, they issued their RFPs.

Except, not everyone played ball. Instead of falling into line on the RFP, one competitive salesperson chose to send a provocative response on why his company would not be participating . . . unless they agreed to a one-on-one meeting with him.

And you know what? It worked.

The sales leader at the CRM company was so confounded by this response that he immediately picked up the phone—and that's exactly what the sales rep wanted in the first place: the conversation, an opportunity to uncover the problems this sales leader was trying to solve and connect with him on a human level. While my company ultimately ended up winning the deal, this vendor who broke the rules wound up being our main competition in the final stages. It's a testament to the power of business conversations.

It's also an important reminder that we can't always sell the way that buyers want to buy; sometimes that would amount to providing a price quote and nothing else. Yes, we always want to facilitate the way buyers want to buy—but first, we have to ensure that they should be buying in the first place.

To do this effectively, salespeople need a framework that elevates their thinking to an executive's level, is flexible enough to accommodate any conversation, and establishes the relationships that facilitate high-level business conversations. They have to not only add value at the end, but throughout the buying cycle to nurture these collaborative relationships—the key to equipping the buyer with the confidence they need to buy.

After all, research shows that impactful business relationships are built on a foundation of trust, credibility and rapport—a topic we'll fully explore in the next chapter.

Put the Pro Back in Sales Professional

4

People Buy from People: Building Credibility, Trust, and Rapport

Sales professionals still face a perception problem.

There's a classic icebreaker that some of our workshop facilitators use at the beginning of sales training sessions because it never fails to get laughs. It's a series of memes showing various perceptions of sellers. On one side of the spectrum, there's an image of a confident professional leading a boardroom presentation, captioned: *What my mom thinks I do*. At the opposite end of the scale, we encounter everyone's worst nightmare of a sleazy salesman, captioned: *What the world thinks I do*.

Why does this unflattering perception persist when the majority of B2B sales organizations embrace buyer-first selling philosophies?

Yes, in the days when sellers controlled the flow of information about products and services, some were less than transparent about the true capabilities of their solutions. Buyers got burned; skepticism skyrocketed.

Then things changed. Today's buyers have a wealth of information they can tap into on demand, eliminating the primary mechanism that enabled the less-than-reputable among us to mislead potential buyers. And yet—that used-car-salesman meme still gets a reaction from everyone in the room. The slide goes up, and laughter ensues. Why do people find that funny? Why do people laugh like that to begin with?

It's a question we've wrestled with as humans for millennia, but at a high level, it's safe to say that laughter is an immediate, unconscious response that has its roots in social interaction. Looking closer at the previous situation, this checks out. It's not uncommon for workshops to be a mix of individuals from across the organization who don't regularly interact. If you're dealing with geographically distributed teams, it might be their first time in a room together. Or you might be dealing with a class of new hires. It's easy to see how an individual in any of those situations would have a vested interest in bonding with the other workshop participants, and so that social cue of laughter is readily picked up and mirrored by everyone in the room, which is exactly what the exercise is designed to do.

The benefits go beyond peer-to-peer bonding. This ice-breaker is also a quick way for the facilitator to begin establishing trust and credibility with the group. But what are they saying with this opener? Yes, they're setting up an us-versus-them mentality—and that involves a tacit acknowledgment that this perception is somewhat valid. On the surface, it's a been-there-felt-that moment—but in a deeper, perhaps unconscious way, we still link that horrible sleazy-salesperson stereotype to the whole selling profession.

Why is that? Why would a room of sophisticated salespeople unconsciously identify their chosen profession with this unsavory stereotype? Fundamentally, no one wants to be sold to. We want to buy, are looking for advisors to facilitate that buying process, and have no interest in sellers who want to make us fit their processes for their benefit.

In the same way that value is customer-specific, so is the reputation of the salesperson. Both must be established on the individual level—every interaction you have with potential buyers is either an opportunity to build credibility, trust and rapport, or to erode it.

Without an authentic human-to-human connection to serve as the foundation for the buying journey, you're going to struggle. Ask yourself: What executive worth their salt is going to divulge critical business challenges to someone they don't trust? And no one trusts an individual whom they perceive to be inauthentic. To become problem experts and have the business conversations that deliver true impact and value, you must present yourself as an authentic, trusted advisor.

The research agrees. My company recently partnered with Training Industry to investigate the disconnect between the behaviors sellers need to succeed and what sales teams actively measure. We surveyed 464 sales leaders and sales enablement decision-makers and found that the most impactful behaviors at each stage of the sales cycle have a common thread running through them: authenticity and strong human-to-human connections. The ability to establish credibility and trustworthiness, as well as to develop and maintain a positive rapport with buyers, is essential to closing deals and building long-term relationships in any selling environment.

And yet, rarely are these qualities measured. While 98% of survey respondents measure their team's sales performance in one way or another, their understanding of sales effectiveness is most often tied to sales outcomes. Only 25% of sales organizations are actively tracking behaviors and behavior development (Figure 4.1).

In this chapter, we'll dive into how salespeople can establish—and maintain—credibility, trust, and rapport throughout the buying cycle and how sales leaders can build these competencies across their teams. Finally, I'll touch on how sales orgs can change their measurement practices to include leading indicators and better track skill development.

Only
25%
of companies
measure sales
behaviors

Figure 4.1   Measuring the Most Impactful Sales Behaviors

Source: Adapted from *The Behaviors That Sales Leaders Care Most About—And How to Measure Them,* ValueSelling Associates, 2021.

Why Should I Listen to You?

As I hinted at in the introduction of this chapter, all successful business relationships are built on a foundation of human-to-human connection and credibility, trust, and rapport. And before you can build those crucial elements, you'll need to get your foot in the door, so let's look at how you can put your best foot forward.

Personal Branding

You're introduced to a professional contact. Where do you go to learn more about this person and if they're credible?

That's right—straight to LinkedIn, which is why it's vital to maintain a well-curated and authentic personal brand. It only makes sense. When prospects are trying to determine whether to accept a meeting with a salesperson and if it is worth their time, viewing their LinkedIn profile is often the first step. In fact, LinkedIn found that salespeople's profiles are viewed at twice the rate of other professionals', and prospects are 87% more likely to accept your InMail if you have a complete and professional profile.[1] Moreover, an earlier study by LinkedIn showed that no social selling action had a greater impact on sales success than the completeness of a seller's LinkedIn profile.[2]

I have learned that buyers spend their time before they spend their money.

Capitalize on this data by taking an inventory of your profile. Does your online brand present you as a credible thought leader, or do you look more like a bot or a job seeker?

Remember, you don't need thousands of followers or posts that go viral. Professionalism and consistency will always win out in the long run. Start with a current, high-quality headshot, a solid description, endorsements from colleagues, and a well-rounded interests section. Then ensure you're engaging with your network: Aim to post three to five times per week, add value in the comments on others' posts, and share your expertise in groups or in longer-form articles. If you're not keen on producing your own content, leveraging third-party content is a low-effort way to demonstrate expertise and establish yourself as a subject matter expert. And it's as easy as picking the two or three points from the article, ebook, or white paper that resonate most with you and posting that along with a call for others to share their reactions.

Show Me That You Know Me

Let me take you back to 1999.

On the morning of January 19, I was walking through the streets of Celebration, Florida, on my way to meet my new boss.

The only way to describe the setting is *surreal*. Built by the Disney Development Corporation in the late 1990s, every element of Celebration was curated to an eerie degree—not even a gum wrapper on the ground. I mean, they even brought in graphic designer Michael Beirut to design every feature that fills its 10 square miles, down to the manhole covers.

At the time, I was running sales training for the leading research and advisory firm, and this was our sales leadership annual kick-off meeting. My company had rented out a movie theater for the occasion. Picture this: You've got 150 anxious sales leaders, from managers to regional vice presidents, packed into a movie theater in the middle of a city that's so manufactured that you are pretty sure even the birds chirping are planned, all waiting for the new boss. Oh, did I mention that this is day two of the event? Due to a visa snafu, our new boss was stuck in the United Kingdom. Here we all are in the audience, staring up at an empty stage when Nigel walks in fresh off an 8-hour flight to set the tone and vision for the entire sales org—and I've never forgotten his opening message. Once he caught his breath and regained his composure, he said: *The customer expects you to show them that you know them, and that's exactly what we're going to do.*

Keep in mind that this was 1999—while the internet existed, the days of detailed information being instantly available were still a decade off. We had an uphill battle to figure out how to do this type of personalization at scale, and we instantly recognized the importance of doing so. If you know the buyer, you can proactively anticipate their needs and ensure you add value with every interaction. Ultimately, personalization was how we won and how we maintained our market position in an increasingly competitive landscape. Nearly 24 years later, it goes to show you: *The more things change, the more they stay the same.*

■ ■ ■

People are drawn to engage with those who understand their point of view. That means putting in the time to do quality research. It all comes down to this: What and who do you think is more credible? Do you want to begin outreach only knowing information like the prospect's title/role and industry news? Or do you want to start with an understanding of their CEO's top three priorities for the year, the company's recent acquisitions or product news, and the likely business challenges on the executive's radar?

The first might get an email opened, but it's a long way from opening the door to an impactful business relationship. To secure that all-important first meeting, you must demonstrate credibility through relevant business knowledge.

The good news is it's never been more time-efficient to put in the work. Many AI-driven tools on the market comb search engines and aggregate vital information such as likely pain points or challenges, recent technology investments, and company news. From there, it's a matter of connecting that researchs to the individual and developing messaging that resonates on a personal level. Imagine their day-to-day: What are their areas of responsibility? What KPIs are they measured on? How do the larger business goals impact their department and job function? What's their competition up to?

Does it really work? And if so, how do you find the time? This is a common refrain. Everyone struggles with top-of-funnel activity—and while most agree in theory that sales outreach should be a highly targeted and personalized experience, their actions say otherwise. Many don't comprehend the power of a personalized, value-added approach and the ability of small actions to pay dividends. For example, the same LinkedIn study mentioned earlier found that potential buyers were 86% more likely to accept your connection request if they noticed you viewed their profile first and 13% more likely to accept if you followed their company. And guess what? Both of those actions add up to less than 1 minute of your time.

Diving into LinkedIn's 2022 State of Sales Report, you'll find further evidence of the power of personalization. The overarching theme of the report is a paradox: While sales tech use exploded during the pandemic—with 91% of sellers at large companies using sales tech at least once per week—top sellers aren't using it to send more emails. They leverage sales tech to be more human, to form better relationships. More than four out of five (89%) of top performers report that they do research "all the time" before reaching out to any prospect. They also tend to spend on average

18% more time updating their CRMs to ensure that key activities are logged across the entire buying committee.[3]

Yes, *it really works.*

The Fiction of Credibility

Think back to the last time you were moved by a movie, TV show, or book. Sure, the cinematography was spectacular and the setting gripping, but what resonated the most? I'm willing to bet it was the story and the characters—and I'll also wager that you saw a little bit of yourself in both.

You'd be forgiven for thinking, *Wait . . . what does this have to do with my sales outreach strategy?*

The answer is a great deal.

As the president and CEO of a sales methodology and training company, it's my job to know what makes high-performing sellers tick and how to instill these attributes across all customer-facing roles within client organizations. With this in mind, my company partnered with Selling Power to survey 154 high-level sales leaders to investigate what sets top performers apart from the pack.

When we asked sales leaders how effective their top sellers are at communicating value, 67% rated their top performers at 8 or higher on a 10-point scale (Figure 4.2).

I've seen this play out time and time again. High-performing reps routinely use value-based stories to captivate, create engagement, and entice busy executives into having meaningful business conversations. The concept of a value-based story is a simple one: It's a 30-second opener that explains how you and your company have helped individuals like the prospect in the past—when done well, it's a sure-fire way to pique interest and establish credibility from the very beginning. A value-based story should relate past successes, clearly demonstrating how your company has solved similar challenges in the past and

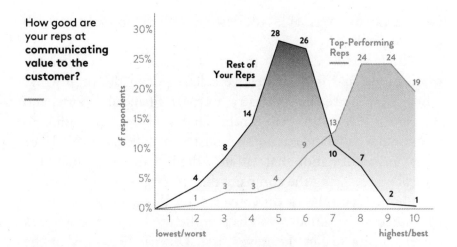

Figure 4.2 Communicating Meaningful Value to Buyers

Source: Adapted from *7 Actionable Habits of Top Performers,* ValueSelling Associates, 2021.

brought similar value or positive outcomes—both personal and professional—to an individual like the potential buyer.

For example, if you're selling a sales tech solution that reduces administrative tasks for sales teams, your value-based story might look like this:

> I've worked with several sales leaders in the aerospace industry, and one company, in particular, was looking for a mechanism to retain top talent. They found that most sellers left because they felt overburdened with administrative tasks and not supported in protecting their selling time.
>
> By partnering with us, they were able to all but eliminate administrative tasks for sales reps, which lead to a 55% increase in time spent selling, employee retention rates above 90%, and a 20% reduction in cost of acquisition.

Notice that there's nothing about the product there—it's all about the customer's likely problems and the measurable impact your company was able to deliver. It's the opposite of an elevator pitch.

The key is focusing on the other person—their challenges, motivations, and goals. Effective sellers put in the prep work: They begin by reading industry journals, financial reports, and the latest LinkedIn post from analyst firms; listening to shareholder calls; and attending industry-specific webinars. They digest any information that will help them better understand the critical issues facing the company they're targeting. By adopting this mindset, you elevate the conversation above the transactional to connect on a human level that's authentic and demonstrates a sincere desire to put the buyer first. Ultimately, you want the prospect to think, "Because I know they've done it elsewhere, I want to have this conversation to leverage their knowledge in helping me solve my problems."

Why Should I Believe You?

In LinkedIn's era-defining *Buyer First* report from 2020, the word "trust" appears again and again—it's more striking when you find a page without it.[4] Three years later, where are we?

It's fair to say we're still firmly set in the age of skeptical and cynical buyers. Havas Group surveyed more than 395,000 individuals worldwide and found that less than half (47%) of brands are seen as trustworthy and that 71% of survey respondents have little faith that brands will make good on their promises.[5] The problem is prospects believe that your success as a sales professional comes at their expense. They think all you really want to do is close the deal and cash your commission check, regardless of whether it's the best thing for them or not—and they're not completely wrong.

Have you experienced similar behavior from sales reps trying to push their products and services? I certainly have—we probably all have, so I don't need to tell you how it feels when that realization hits you, and you start adding up what it's going to cost you to fix your mistake. So the question becomes: How can we put these fears to rest for our prospects?

Building trust is a three-step process that involves authenticity, follow-through, and empathy.

Authenticity

A recent Bain & Company survey found that 92% of B2B buyers prefer virtual sales interactions—that's a whopping 17% increase from the survey conducted in May 2020.[6] Clearly, virtual selling isn't going away, and yet, we still struggle with authenticity in this environment.

However, we can also use the unique situation of work-from-home culture to our advantage. After all, what's more authentic than a window into someone's home?

Use it to your advantage by starting with your background. Ditch the slick bookshelf that's carefully stocked with every best-selling business book printed over the last decade in favor of something more authentic. Insert tokens from your personal life to give prospects a window into who you are. If you're an avid golfer, this might be a marker from your favorite course or a trophy from a club match. If you're a sailing enthusiast, it could be a model of your boat. An endurance athlete might include a framed bib from his or her biggest race. You get the idea—small, personal touches.

The most important aspect here is the difference between engineered and manufactured: While engineering your environment to share more of yourself will build trust, manufacturing an environment and a Zoom persona to match will erode it.

The same can be said about your LinkedIn presence. Don't be afraid to put your personal spin on the content you're sharing. Instead of merely sharing your company's latest post, share it and highlight the points that resonated with you or film a 2-minute video of you discussing how you've seen its themes play out in your day-to-day.

Now, you don't have to take a week of personal time off to set this mechanism up. It's easy to create a program for championing the success of your customers that easily fits into your daily routine. For instance, there's a field rep at one of our payroll clients who sells to small businesses. As part of his monthly workflow, he's on the road, checking in with clients and ensuring that they're seeing the measurable value they expected. On his latest tour, he took it upon himself to print customer-specific appreciation certificates and present them to all his clients. And he made sure to take photos of the occasion so that when he was back at his hotel that night, he could post the photos to LinkedIn, tag the business, and sing their praises. Not only did his clients absolutely love the free publicity, but it did wonders for showcasing the diversity of his customers and bringing him more business from new types of accounts.

In short, to be successful, be real. Creating original content that highlights your personality and shows your desire to always put the buyer first and celebrate customer success is transformative. It builds your personal brand and lays the groundwork for a trusting relationship.

Accurate Follow-through

In contrast to credibility, the tricky thing about trust is that it's built incrementally. Trust fluctuates according to actions. The easiest way to ensure that prospects continue to trust you is to ensure you're doing what you said you'd do and in a timely manner.

Imagine this: You've had a brilliant first sales call and told a credibility story that convincingly illustrated how you and your company have helped similar prospects in the past. All that's left to do is summarize your conversation in a follow-up note and provide the requested materials: a case study and a piece of collateral that includes information on how your solution integrates with the prospective buyer's tech stack.

It's an easy ask, and it better be—you only have 12 minutes to put this email together before your next meeting. Except, when you send over the case study, you send the one pertaining to your client in health care, not the one in the pharmaceutical industry.

The prospect opens the email and immediately wonders: *Do they know my business at all? Do they actually have my best interest in mind?*

It's a slight misstep. Everyone makes mistakes. Still, blunders in client communications can be difficult to bounce back from. Every time you accurately deliver on what was promised in a timely fashion, trust goes up. Every time you miss the mark, trust falls and must be rebuilt.

You don't have to get everything perfect all the time, but putting in the extra effort to accurately follow through on client-facing tasks is well worth it.

Empathy

Empathy is the foundational skill that makes all of the above effective. People will always be the most important aspect of any complex sales process—and when you're able to authentically connect at a human level, a strong business relationship is forged. Conversely, if you feign interest and empathy, it will show, and the prospect will disengage—particularly executives who are notorious for guarding their time.

Our research bears this notion out: Looking back to the study conducted in partnership with Selling Power, we see that the majority of respondents rated their top sellers' ability to be empathetic to buyers' challenges at 8 or above on a 10-point scale (Figure 4.3).

One of the most effective ways to convey empathy is to exhibit a healthy curiosity and actively listen to the prospect. It sounds simple. It sounds like common sense—but common sense isn't always common practice.

To engage at a high level, salespeople must learn to listen with curiosity instead of listening merely to reply. It's being truly

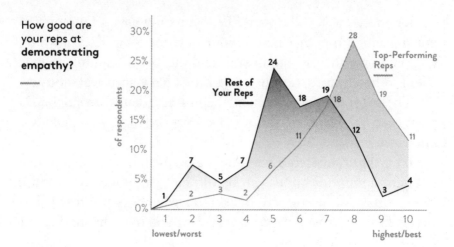

Figure 4.3 Empathizing with the Buyer's Position, Problems, and Goals

Source: Adapted from *7 Actionable Habits of Top Performers,* ValueSelling Associates, 2021.

curious about the prospect's situation; asking the questions that further high-level business conversations; and confirming to build a match between problem, solution, and future value realization. Here again, the research speaks volumes: In the same study mentioned previously, the overwhelming majority of sales leaders rated their top reps 7 out of 10 in listening skills, with nearly 70% rating them 8 or higher (Figure 4.4).

Unfortunately, many sales leaders make the mistake of thinking that soft skills like active listening cannot be taught; that's not my experience. It's both possible and extremely beneficial to cultivate these skills across the sales organization. You can get a baseline of where your team stands by reviewing your team's sales calls and listening:

- Do they tend to reserve questions only for the initial discovery phase or do they weave targeted questions into every sales call?
- Do they stick to tried-and-true questions about the company and problems, or are they genuinely curious and spontaneous

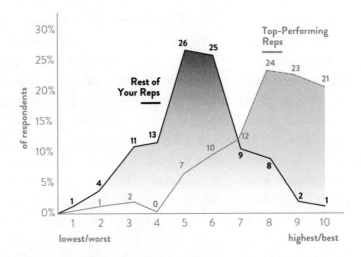

Figure 4.4 The Value of Intentional Questioning and Active Listening

Source: Adapted from *7 Actionable Habits of Top Performers,* ValueSelling Associates, 2021.

throughout the conversation? Are they able to adjust their approach in real time?

For salespeople, the best way to improve is to let your conversational intelligence do the heavy lifting. Challenge yourself to be fully present and focus on every word the prospect is saying and their unique word choices—using the same word choices that the prospect uses is one of the preliminary steps to building a strong rapport.

Why Should I Take the Next Meeting?

People do business with people they like: According to LinkedIn's 2021 *State of Sales* report, 43% of buyers said having a "favorable impression of the sales professional" would make them more likely to select their company as a vendor.[7]

And that's doubly true when you enter the inevitable negotiation stage: Our research study, *The Behaviors and Skills*

Sales Leaders Care Most About—And How to Measure Them, asked sales leaders to rank the most important skills at each stage of the sales cycle, and 48% identified "maintaining rapport with buyers" to be the most crucial. How do you build it?

Again, it all comes down to putting the spotlight on the customer and being proactive and flexible. Start by paying attention to the prospect's body language, tone, and style. One of the most effective ways to build and maintain rapport is to match the prospect when appropriate. If they're leaning in, you want to lean in. If they speak quickly, with high energy, take their lead and follow suit. Most importantly, pay attention to the word choices they're making and mirror that back to them. It's a fantastic way to make someone feel heard and can augment your credibility, especially if you're selling into a new market or a new type of customer.

Like so many things in sales, a well-developed understanding of the prospect is paramount. Remember: It is essential to record the highlights from each conversation in the system of record. Every conversation is an opportunity to learn more and align your solution with this individual's personal and professional motivations. After all, if you understand what the prospect values on both a professional and personal level, it enables you to be proactive, anticipate their needs, and add value even when they're not asking you to.

Measuring the Behaviors That Build Credibility, Trust, and Rapport

It's one thing to identify the right behaviors, and a whole different struggle to accurately measure these efforts so your sales teams can continually improve. Going back to the study, *The Behaviors and Skills Sales Leaders Care Most About—And How to Measure*

Them, we found a shocking disconnect: While 98% of respondents did some type of measurement, their understanding of sales effectiveness was most often tied to coaching reports and supervisor ratings—only 25% were directly measuring most sales behaviors.

The danger here is that, despite our best efforts to stay completely objective, coaching reports are influenced by manager-rep dynamics, and even the most objective are based on limited data. This is not a comment on the sales manager's effectiveness, but more a reality of the situation. It might sound counterintuitive; however, to accurately measure the selling behaviors that build authentic business relationships, lean into your tech stack.

Credibility

In the first stage of the sales cycle, the majority of sales leaders rated "establishing credibility and trustworthiness" as the most important skill. Are you using conversational intelligence to analyze the first few minutes of initial sales calls? If you're teaching your sellers to deliver value-based, credibility stories, they should appear here. Start tracking how frequently and to what effect your sellers are able to deliver a 30-second engaging story in that opening sequence.

Trustworthiness

As face-to-face interactions continue to be limited, maintaining a trustworthy online presence is critical. A fast audit of your sales teams' profiles can be revealing. Work with marketing and/or enablement to provide easy-to-implement strategies and assets that sales professionals can leverage to increase the professionalism and consistency of their online presence.

Rapport

Dive into that CRM data. What notes are sellers leaving on their opportunities? I'd expect detailed notes on the organization's problems: why your solution is the best match, the expected ROI, and how those both map to business drivers—but there should also be that ever-important personal angle. What's in it for the buyer themselves?

Value is measured in the eye of the beholder, and if sellers do not establish the rapport that allows them to uncover personal value, they're not truly differentiated. As a result, the opportunity is at risk.

■ ■ ■

We've all met those magnetic sellers—the rainmakers who are able to elicit a "yes" from prospects no matter the state of the economy or their territory. While it's tempting to view these top performers as "born" salespeople, our research disagrees. It's the fundamental, soft skills that are responsible for building relationships and instilling confidence in buying decisions.

Ultimately, each stage of the sales cycle is an opportunity for sales professionals to establish and build credibility, trust, and rapport with customers. To maximize their impact, you must connect your data to the selling behaviors that will drive sustainable sales results.

5

Think Like an Executive

Kate has a call scheduled for next week that could make or break her quarter.

It's been weeks in the making. Finally, after working with a large team of committed managers to solve a customer-service problem, she has an opportunity to meet with Andrea, the CFO responsible for making the final decision.

Now what? How will this meeting be different than the countless other meetings she has had with department heads and team leaders? How will the conversation contrast with every other sales call she has made?

She knows three things are table stakes:

1. She has to demonstrate that she understands her *business*.

2. She has to add relevance to the conversation and bring insight.

3. She has to earn the right to continue the conversation *and* further advance the opportunity.

Fantastic! Except, how does she actually accomplish these things, and where should she start?

■ ■ ■

Every company has various levels of decision-makers and decision-influencers, each with different perspectives and roles in the buying process. At times, you'll meet with the individuals who use your products and services. Other times, you're talking to the individuals who create specifications and product requirements but don't actually use the products themselves. And then there are those magic moments: the times when you have the privilege of speaking with the executives who lead those teams and will ultimately have the authority to make and execute a buying decision.

These senior executives handle the larger, strategic issues facing the company, and their opinions carry an enormous impact throughout the organization. As a result, communicating with executives is a whole different game—a high-stakes one that often sales professionals find intimidating.

Why is that?

For starters, executives speak a fundamentally different language than the end users and have a wildly different perspective. They may not even care about your products—just the impact of your products on their business. To influence an executive, it is critical to demonstrate your understanding of their role and what is important to them. And that starts and ends with business acumen: the vital component that transforms salespeople from peddler to peer.

At its core, business acumen is a keenness in understanding and the ability to deal with a business situation in an efficient manner that will likely lead to a good outcome. To some, it is financial literacy. In my experience, it's much more.

Business acumen has two key components. The first element is executive-level strategic thinking, the ability to see the big picture and understand the motivations, goals, and objectives of any organization. Executive-level thinking enables executives to separate the important issues from the noise. It's an act of synthesis that acts as the foundation for how they spend resources, including time. Not only is this type of analysis critical for innovation and problem-solving, but it also builds decisiveness and confidence. Ultimately, it is the ability to synthesize and understand the moving forces behind macro trends and implement micro actions within your company.

The second component embodied in business acumen is financial literacy. Whether we like it or not, finance/accounting is the language of business. In the end, every buying decision is a business decision, so let's look at these two factors from Kate's point of view.

Understanding Executive Prospects

Almost every sales professional has automation that can spoon-feed them data on key industry trends and updates from prospects' companies. However, the alert does us no good if we don't understand the implications, importance, and relevance of that information. We are required to turn that data into insight that furthers our understanding. To do that, we need to think like a senior executive thinks; we must also read what they read.

Senior executives spend their time and attention thinking about issues with far-reaching consequences—this includes economics, global markets, Wall Street, government regulations, industry dynamics, and social issues. Understanding and becoming conversant in the elements that have the power to shift markets helps you establish your credibility and relevance.

Start with the high-level context for your prospect: targeted research on their industry, company and, in some cases, regional affairs. Seek out industry associations that you can join and learn from. Identify and subscribe to industry publications, blogs/newsletters, and podcasts from the target executive's industry. Stay abreast of the macro industry trends for your executive. Are they in a regulated industry? Are there global issues facing the executive and his organization? If so, how could these shape priorities and decisions?

A company's website is often the next source of clues. Press releases, biographies, news, and events are a good starting point. If the company is public, look to the investor relations section of its website and search out financial reports, executive summaries, and quarterly calls. If it's a private company, data sources like Crunchbase and Dun and Bradstreet are a good place to start.

From here, head straight to LinkedIn and follow the company and the executive. What groups are they a part of? What companies do they follow? What types of content do they engage with, comment on, or post? Join or subscribe where relevant and ensure you're reading the most recent posts, gathering insights, and looking for trends. After all, an executive's LinkedIn activity paints an accurate picture of the types of topics and peers that this individual chooses to spend his or her precious time intersecting with.

Be sure to let them know you're researching them too. Most make the mistake of having their settings locked down, but you want executives to know you viewed their profile. As I mentioned last chapter, LinkedIn found that potential buyers were 86% more likely to accept your InMail if they noticed you viewed their profile first—making this an easy prospecting tip well worth your time.[1] Simply go to "Setting and Privacy" under your account info and select "Visibility," then "Profile viewing options" to control what the user sees when you view their profile.

And don't forget the most important question: *Do you have mutual connections?*

■ ■ ■

Not long ago, I was preparing for an executive meeting with a new prospect. As I reviewed his LinkedIn profile, I learned he was connected to a former boss at a previous employer, which was excellent news since he and I have a strong relationship. I picked up the phone and called my former manager.

Turns out, my boss was actually the prospect's neighbor. Their kids were great friends, and they spent time together on weekends, hopping between the various community sporting events their children were involved in. My former boss was able to provide me with a bit of advice on my prospect's communication style and preferences—the executive in question was direct, very direct. He had a notorious dislike for salespeople who wasted his time with niceties and became visitors, not peer professionals who added value. This knowledge proved invaluable as I prepped for the call and made a tremendous difference in helping me quickly establish trust and rapport.

Speaking an Executive's Language

Your role is not to pitch—it's to ask insightful questions that ignite a value-added conversation. Because guess what? The executive does not care one bit about your product. That's right! They could care less about features and functionality—all the bells and whistles and data-packed dashboards you put in front of them will likely fail to elicit the slightest response.

I know, that may be a hard pill to swallow, and it is the reality of the situation. The executive cares about their own issues and how they're going to lead their company to success. Simply put, they're there to make business decisions and execute on them.

The disconnect is that most sales reps spend their time in training learning about their products. When they're anxious or excited or unsure of what to say next or how to engage a tough prospect, they fall back to a product-centric approach. Executives don't care. They want to understand the positive impact you can provide—the *how* behind this isn't really of interest to them. To engage on this level, your expertise must be broader than your product knowledge with this approach. The value you will bring is not merely the outcomes you are selling but the experience an executive has when communicating with you. With your research and expertise, you can share novel, actionable ideas that expand an executive's thinking—but only if you speak the same language.

Financial Literacy

"Accounting is the language of business" is a quote commonly attributed to Warren Buffet. When asked by a young intern at CNBC for advice on how to make it in the business world, Buffet answered that he should study accounting as a language, as if he were studying a foreign language. Equipped with that knowledge, the intern would be able to read financial statements and become conversant in the fundamentals of the business world.

Financial statements and accounting are how companies keep score, and every single business is in the habit of scorekeeping: not-for-profits, health care, privately held companies, publicly traded companies, educational entities, and even government agencies. They all use accounting to measure the efficacy of their resource management within the organization. While there may be slight regional differences and differences in language, accounting is essentially global in nature, and the principles apply to all organizations. In turn, it's the universal principle that enables executives to justify decisions and track their financial impact.

As a sales professional, it's vital for you to understand the fundamentals of finance and accounting. Ultimately, you will be asking this executive to make a business decision to purchase your product or service, i.e., to justify the investment based on the language of finance—so let's look at what you need to know.

You should be comfortable navigating three standard financial statements:

1. Income statement or profit and loss
2. Balance sheet
3. Statement of cash flows

All three of these financial instruments are related, yet provide very different information.

Income Statement   The income statement or profit and loss statement (P&L) memorializes how much money was made, spent, and kept over a period. Most organizations capture their income statement on an annual and quarterly basis. In some cases, they may even look at the income statement monthly.

At its highest level, Revenue – Expenses = Income.

There is also a subset of profit and loss that is calculated before the following expenses: tax, depreciation, and amortization. That calculation is known as EBITDA (earnings before interest, taxes, depreciation, and amortization)—it accounts for variability across regions and types of assets. For instance, taxes could differ significantly due to the location of the business, and depreciation and amortization are noncash expenses.

Quick win: An efficient way to analyze the P&L is to look at year-over-year (YOY) of the following:

- Total revenue growth rate
- Net income growth rate
- Profit margin growth rate

Balance Sheet   In contrast to the income statement, the balance sheet is a snapshot of a point in time, one that's typically compared with previous periods or snapshots. It's indicative of the overall health of the business and contains a picture of the assets and liabilities of an entity on a single date. Assets are what the company owns and can include cash on hand, inventory, accounts receivable or property such as capital equipment, real estate, or vehicles. In contrast, liabilities are what the company owes, including all outstanding debt and accounts payable. The third component of the balance sheet is owner equity. By definition, the assets, liabilities, and owner equity are in balance: Assets = Liabilities + Owner Equity

Think of the balance sheet as an organization's yearly physical. Is it healthy? Are assets growing based on the balance sheet snapshots over time? Has debt or liabilities increased?

Quick win: To determine the health of a business at a glance, pay attention to the following:

- A healthy company will show Net Cash Provided by Operating Activities as increasing over time.
- Look at Net Cash from Financing Activities and consider the age of the company you're researching to analyze how it borrows cash.
- Generally, it should have at least 10% of its overall money in cash, but check what is typical for the industry.

Cash Flow Statement   The final financial statement is the cash flow statement—the bridge between the income statement and the balance sheet that demonstrates the sources of cash and the outlays of cash. Think of this one like you would your bank statement. Like the profit-and-loss statement, the cash flow statement is for a defined period of time. As you can see in Figure 5.1, it begins with an opening balance and details sources of cash and uses of cash to reveal the ending balance.

Quick win: Identify trends by investigating the following:

- Assets to sales trends. If sales grow, assets should grow. If sales are down, assets should also be down.
- Liabilities to sales trends. If sales grow, liabilities grow. If sales are down, liabilities should also decrease.

Of course, nothing happens in a vacuum, and that's where ratios come in. Ratios can tell you how profitable a company is and in all of the following ratios, the higher the percentage, the

Opening balance

+ Sources of cash (deposits):

+ Sales
+ Loans/Debt
+ Owner Equity or Capital Contributions
+ Interest income

– Uses of cash (withdrawals):

- Operating Expenses
- Investment Expenses - for example interest
- Investing Expenses - dividends or owner distributions

 Ending balance

Figure 5.1   Cash Flow Statement

better. Comparing the resulting ratios to the averages in your potential buyer's industry gives you a preliminary understanding of how it stacks up against the competition. Pay particular attention to the following:

- Equity Ratio > 30%. For example, an equity ratio divides the equity number by the total assets. The resulting percentage should be 30% or greater. Check comparable companies in your buyer's industry.
- Current Ratio > 1%. Another useful ratio is to divide current assets by current liabilities. The result should be greater than 1, meaning trends are good and growing.

- Asset Utilization Ratios. Asset utilization is a category of ratios used by business analysts to determine how well a company is using its available assets to generate a profit. Following are some examples:
  - Inventory Turnover = Cost of Goods Sold divided by Inventories
  - Return on Assets (ROA) = Net Income divided by Assets
  - Return on Equity (ROE) = Net Income divided by Total Shareholder's Equity

Why Care

The objective of developing financial literacy is *not* to become a financial analyst; it is to spot the trends that could be the foundation for the executive doing or expanding business with you.

One of the fundamental principles we espouse is: *People need a reason to change.* In preparing for an executive sales call, your objective is to ultimately connect your product, service or solution to their corporate objectives and initiatives. And the clues that unravel the mystery of those business objectives are revealed by understanding the financials.

Since the beginning of professional B2B sales, sellers understood that if they wanted their solution to be relevant, they first needed to understand and confirm what problem or problems they can solve. Every organization has problems—and not every problem will warrant an investment to fix it. Some problems are simply worth living with. Either there's no clear upside to fixing it, or it's not a big enough nuisance to make a real difference. Ultimately, businesses determine which problems are worth solving based on whether that problem has a significant impact on a key corporate objective or not. C-suite executives allocate time, energy, and resources to the business issues that they recognize and focus on. Everything else—at least in the short term—is a nice-to-have rather than a critical business need.

For example, if a company is focused on improving its bottom line, executives have two high-level options. Option one is to increase their revenue. Strategies for doing so might include a number of different tactics and initiatives: They could raise their prices, create new products, enter new markets, or merge with another company. Option two is to reduce expenses, including moves like vendor consolidation or elimination, layoffs, divesting of various businesses, or discontinuing support for outdated products.

As a sales professional, it's imperative that you're able to demonstrate how your product or service contributes to the business issues, not the extent of its technical capabilities. The purpose of the executive sales call is to confirm the context for your products or services from the executive's point of view. Demonstrating your understanding of their industry, their company, and the executive themself enables you to prepare relevant stories or anecdotes to establish credibility. It also provides the foundation for predicting business initiatives and equips you with a powerful ally: *intrigue.*

Where to Look   Now that you're convinced of the efficacy of this approach, you might be thinking: *How do I get started?* Your biggest ally is the annual report. Even if you only have 15 minutes, focusing on the following three elements is enough to help you create compelling messaging and questions that establish your credibility.

1. The CEO's letter: Make no mistake, this has been polished and polished again for public consumption, but the priorities haven't changed.

2. Financial statements and supplementary data: Can you spot the trends? Is the company currently growing or not growing?

3. Risk factors: They've already assessed the threats to their business—what types of problems are they likely facing as a result?

Identifying the Specifics   Now, let's put this to work for you. As you prepare for your next executive sales call, work through the following checklist to ensure you're prepared with insights that will pique their interest.

High-level Company Info
- What's the company's business?
- What are its products and services?
- How do they go to market?
- Who are its customers?
- What are the drivers or trends about it in the press?
- Describe its movement in the market.
- Any recent changes in the industry or for your buyer?
- Are there notable challenges or problems in its industry?
- What about industry opportunities or threats?

Financials
- What's its fiscal year and how could this impact budget cycles?
- How have revenues changed over the past few years?
- How have profit margins changed?
- How have net profits changed?
- Calculate the percentages for profit margins and net income.
- As you analyze the revenue, profit margins, and net income, what do the numbers suggest to you about the company's financial health?

6

Mastering Sales Conversations: Asking the Right Questions, at the Right Time

If there's anyone who knows how to conduct an interview, it's Oprah Winfrey. She makes it look effortless, and hiding behind that easygoing facade is rigorous intentionality.

Oprah has a singular way of shaping interviews that tackle tough topics and leverage provocative questions to create intrigue and uncover surprising information—yet she still manages to do this in a way that feels collaborative and conversational. As sales professionals, this mix of deliberate questioning and collaboration is our ultimate goal: We must uncover the information we need to validate if we're the right fit *and* collaborate with the potential buyer to select and implement the right solution.

Don't Question the Value of Good Questions

Think back to the last time you went to dinner with a good friend.

You likely recall the restaurant and the food, the little sensory details like the man twirling the neon green sign outside the carwash across the street or the squawking birds in the background.

But what about the first meal you shared together—what can you recall? Suddenly, it's much more difficult to remember the details that paint a vivid scene—but I'm willing to bet there's one thing you do remember: the conversation.

I'm also willing to bet it wasn't a monologue. You likely exhibited a genuine curiosity about the other person; the conversation naturally flowed from question to answer and back again; and you probably talked about more than the weather, covering various ideas, problems, possible solutions, and the motivations behind solving those problems.

Those are the types of conversations that build authentic human-to-human connections and win more business.

Our recent research studies have all come to the same conclusion:

- When we asked sales leaders what the most essential behavior for prospecting and qualifying leads in virtual selling was, 56% agreed that it all comes down to "asking good questions and active listening." (See Figure 6.1.)
- As I mentioned in Chapter 4, sales leaders agree that top performers recognize the importance of asking relevant, targeted questions throughout every sales conversation to gain a deeper understanding of the customer's point of view. When asked to rate them on a 10-point scale, the overwhelming majority gave their top performers a rating of 8 or higher (Figure 6.2).

Clearly, thoughtful inquiry and active listening go a long way toward separating top performers from the rest of the pack. And there's a persistent misconception here: Many believe you cannot teach these skills. I'm here to tell you that they can be taught—and you'll need a strategic approach that breaks the desired behaviors into their component parts and shows you how to organically insert this into your existing sales habits.

Essential Sales Behaviors for Prospecting/Qualifying Leads in Virtual Selling

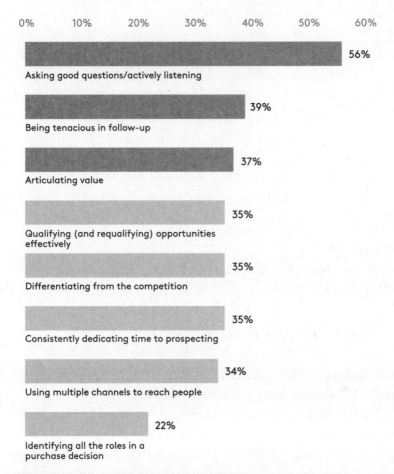

Figure 6.1 The Most Impactful Prospecting and Qualifying Behaviors

Source: Adapted from *The Behaviors That Sales Leaders Care Most About—And How to Measure Them,* ValueSelling Associates, 2021.

Luckily, that's what this chapter is all about. In it, we'll cover open, probe, confirm (O-P-C) questions and anxiety questions, how to structure them, and common traps to avoid. Finally, we'll look at how to use them in your actual sales calls.

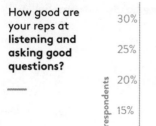

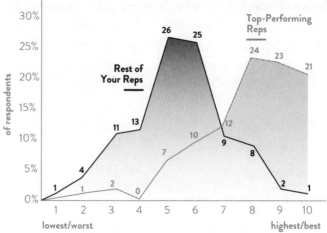

Figure 6.2 The Value of Intentional Questioning and Active Listening

Source: Adapted from *7 Actionable Habits of Top Performers,* ValueSelling Associates, 2021.

The O-P-C Questioning Technique

You've heard the saying, "Curiosity killed the cat." What about "Curiosity helped the sales rep make president's club"?

Unlike the fabled, unlucky cat, in B2B sales, being genuinely curious rarely gets you into trouble. In fact, conveying curiosity through intentional questioning and active listening builds business relationships by demonstrating interest and elevating the conversation above the transactional.

The key is to be genuine in your interest and consultative in your approach and remember that this is not a linear process but an organic, cyclical one. To ensure you truly understand the potential buyer's issues, business problems, priorities, and motivations, you'll need to master O-P-C questions—open-ended, probing, and confirming questions—so let's look at how they break down.

Open-ended When you pick up a good friend at the airport whom you haven't seen in a while, how does the conversation go? In my experience, it's typically punctuated by open-ended questions: *How are you? How's your family? How is work going?* You're curious about your friend. You want to get her talking, to hear about her situation, her challenges, successes, and goals. And it's the same for business conversations.

Open-ended questions facilitate high-level business conversations by encouraging expansive answers. Since these types of questions cannot be answered by a *yes* or *no* response, they enable you to gain crucial insight into a prospect's thinking. Often, *how* they choose to respond, and *where* they start are as powerful as the substance of the answer itself.

While it's tempting to cram as much nuance into questions as possible to demonstrate your knowledge, the best questions are also the simplest ones. Avoid complex questions. You never want to presuppose anything, set up a dichotomy of choice, or lead the prospect in any way. This technique is about information gathering in its purest form. If you listen carefully, you'll also learn the unique word choices they employ and be one step closer to building a strong rapport.

Probing Probing questions lead the prospective buyer on a journey of self-discovery to explore the business issue from all angles. Here's your chance to drill down further, uncover challenges and how these connect to business drivers, and determine the value that the right solution will provide. Probing questions often result in "yes" or "no" answers and are meant to clarify. Don't be afraid to hear "no," either. It's all about respectful persistence and formulating a mutual understanding of which problems are worth solving.

These questions can also be used to subtly challenge and expand a prospect's thinking without creating friction and help you understand how prospects prioritize problems—enabling you to reorder these so the problems you can uniquely solve are at the top of the list.

Confirming Once you believe you've identified those impactful issues and solutions, test your accuracy. This is your opportunity to show the prospect that they have been _heard_. Here's where those active listening skills pay off. Be sure to mirror the prospect's terminology when confirming business issues and motivations. It's the vital component to building empathy and ensuring you're both on the same page. While these types of questions are necessary, it can feel awkward at first to use them since confirming questions aren't typically employed in most social settings.

Anxiety Questions

I'll let you in on a little secret: I'm a _big_ sports fan.

For me, it's utterly fascinating to watch elite athletes excel despite tremendous pressure, and there's no better example than Olympic track and field athletes.

One false start can send a sprinter or hurdler home. That's all it takes to destroy more than 4 years of labor and dedication—and yet, these phenomenal athletes come back after another 4 years of hard work. And it's not good enough to merely come back. They have to be stronger and tougher each time.

I'm intrigued by world-class athletes' demand to continually change for the better, since, as humans, we're hardwired to resist change because it introduces anxiety. Yet at the prompting of a coach or another trusted advisor, athletes manage to navigate change efficiently.

It's the same for B2B sales. No matter what you're selling, you're selling change. In some cases, that change has the potential to make or break organizations and the buyers who are responsible. Still, if anxiety is inherent to the process, then it's not necessarily a negative element—it's one we can use to our advantage if we're careful.

Anxiety questions allow us to disrupt a prospect's thought process and prompt them to address the unacknowledged consequences of maintaining the status quo. Anxiety questions are provocative and can even be challenging. They are designed to disrupt the thought pattern of a prospect. At a high level, these are the *What if . . .* questions you'll fall back on to engage overconfident buyers and jump-start a stalled sales process. In the next sections, we'll look at how and when to use these in conjunction with O-P-C questions.

How to Use the O-P-C Questioning Technique

Over the course of my sales career, I've been trained in various methodologies. Most are very good at telling you what you need to know about an opportunity, but few tell you how to go about getting that information in the first place.

O-P-C questioning fills that gap. It's the catalyst that activates value-based selling and provides a conversational cadence that allows you to deepen your understanding of the prospect's situation and develop an understanding of where the opportunity is going. The power of this technique is its applicability—in a world where salespeople are having more conversations with more stakeholders, O-P-C questioning provides the framework for facilitating *all* of those conversations. Sure, the content will change, but the method is always the same.

Because you'll use the same questioning framework to engage every decision-maker, it enables you to understand the buying process from all angles, including every role that can influence the decision—a vital piece of knowledge that's often overlooked by even senior sales reps.

■ ■ ■

The true magic of this questioning cadence is learning to switch between question types seamlessly until you have identified a business driver that your solution will impact in a meaningful and measurable way. That takes practice—and there's certainly no shame in stacking the deck in your favor.

Lean into your research to prepare five to seven open-ended questions that will help you identify problems already on the prospect's radar and how those issues impact the business and solutions your product is uniquely qualified to provide. Now, don't rattle these off like a nervous understudy in the school play.

In the end, you might only ask a few of the questions in their prepared form. The idea is to help you envision the possible avenues the conversation could take ahead of time—freeing you up to place all of your attention on the other human.

Quality research enables you to come prepared with the types of relevant questions that simultaneously showcase your expertise and invite prospects to deepen their thinking on any given issue—but it's the flow of conversation that will uncover the information you need to establish a match between prospects' understanding of an ideal solution and your company's offerings.

Perhaps you're working for a company that sells software designed to facilitate sales coaching; example open-ended questions might include the following:

- *I see that your company recently made the decision to hire more hybrid sales reps. How have your managers adapted their face-to-face coaching practices to this new work environment?*

- *How is this new method of coaching impacting seller behaviors?*
- *In your opinion, what are you doing to improve your manager's sales coaching abilities?*

The next step is to take the basis of the answers to these questions and probe for more information. To see how that might play out, let's expand on the previous example:

- Open-ended question: *How is this new method of coaching impacting seller behaviors?*
- Prospect's response: *It's difficult to say. There's no clear correlation between the number of coaching conversations and rep performance. Plus, it's hard to pin down what actually happens during these sessions.*
- Probing question: *Is that because there's no standardized structure for coaching conversations and reports?*

The hypothetical rep in this example uses a probing question to gather more information about the company's coaching practices *and* subtly steer the conversation in the direction of possible solutions, solutions the company's offering is well-situated to provide.

Skipping further along in the conversation, you'd arrive at an opportunity to confirm your understanding. It would look something like this: *What I'm hearing is that sales managers don't have the structure they need to effectively coach, and second-line managers don't have a way to efficiently review the substance of coaching conversations—did I get that right?*

Here's where things get interesting. The prospect might agree, he might disagree, or he might agree with a caveat. It's common to hear: *Oh, I did say that, but thinking about it more, I'd add ____.* By synthesizing prospects' responses and playing them back to them, you provide an easy way for prospects to examine their own thinking, which often results in a reordering of priorities or the addition of previously missed information. This cyclical structure of open-probe-confirm allows multiple opportunities for this type of clarification and deepening of the discussion. And since you're the one helping them to think about problems in new ways, it builds your credibility and relevance.

It's vital to remember that none of this works if you're not actively listening and taking notes on key points. Yes, conversational intelligence will do the heavy lifting post-call, but when you're in the middle of it, jotting down key phrases and word choices by hand is vital to building rapport. No, you read that right, "by hand." I hear you—you're probably thinking: *But Julie, I type so much faster than I write. Why does the method matter?* It matters because it will help you better remember those crucial details. Without taking notes, I cannot accurately ask confirming questions during the call or meeting.

According to a study by Pam Mueller and Daniel Oppenheimer,[1] students who wrote out notes by hand learned more than those who typed them. Sure, the laptop writers won out in the volume category, but the hand-writers walked away with significantly stronger conceptual understandings of the material presented.

Speaking of developing a strong conceptual understanding of the prospect's situation, what exactly do you need to know? Use this checklist to help guide your use of the O-P-C questioning technique.

Problem

- What are the problems the prospect is dealing with?
- What's causing these problems?
- How do these problems impact the business objectives?

Solution

- What does the prospect believe to be the ideal solution?
- How will that solution impact the business?
- What competing solutions are being considered?

Value

- What quantified impact will solving the problem provide to the business?
- What's the quantified impact of not solving the problem?
- Is that quantified impact enough to motivate urgency and bring about change?
- What's in it for the prospect?

Power/Decision-Maker

- Who is involved in the buying decision?
- Who has the power to sign the purchase order?
- Will other departments need to review the final contract?
- When can you meet with everyone involved?

Plan

- What next steps are the prospect recommending?
- Is a proof of concept or ROI analysis needed?
- If your solution is the ideal fit, is there anything else that could get in the way of moving forward?

How to Use Anxiety Questions

Anxiety questions are a versatile wildcard. Use them throughout the sales process whenever you need a provocative approach to shake things up or a path to new dialogues.

For example, you're talking to an executive who has grown complacent—somehow, her earlier interest has disappeared, and it's difficult to tell if she even believes she's potentially at risk to miss her business objective. This is the ideal moment for a carefully phrased anxiety question. Let's say you sell network security solutions. You might ask something along the lines of: *I saw that your competitor SkyLabs has been in the news recently for the*

$4.2-million settlement of its data breach last fall. Have you thought about how a potential lawsuit might affect your ability to hit your cost-containment goals?

Or maybe you're working an opportunity whose progress has slowed to the pace of the beltway at rush hour. Soon enough, you get hit with a stalling tactic you were expecting: *Love to do it, but now's not good—let's push off the start until next quarter.* To create urgency, refocus the conversation on value. In this example, you might say, *I understand, and I'm concerned that delaying implementation will put your outcomes at risk. What happens if you're not able to hit your revenue goals by year end?*

The previous examples only scratch the surface of the anxiety question's versatility. At a high level, anxiety questions can be used anytime you need prospects to recognize something they're not recognizing today—anytime you need prospects to sit back and ask themselves, *Did I miss something?*

Use this tactic to uncover business issues or bring the consequences of inaction to light and prompt urgency. Anxiety questions are also extremely useful for disrupting a client's view of a solution. For instance, in the sales methodology space, not all solutions are streamlined—some are potent, yet incredibly complex, to the point where they're notoriously difficult for salespeople to adopt. When I'm up against a competitor whose methodology I know to be particularly cumbersome, I'll bring up the past experiences of former clients: *We've had clients who've gone through X and struggled with adoption. What would the damage to your organization be if you spent X on training and no one executed it?*

Remember: Above all, never risk your rapport with the prospect.

Anxiety questions are powerful tools, but only if you're able to be provocative while being respectful. That's a difficult line for many salespeople to find and walk, especially if you're new to an industry or a particular sales role. Be honest with yourself: Have you built enough expertise and emotional intelligence to ask these questions? If you're not sure, that's okay. It's not uncommon for reps to bring managers or subject matter experts (SMEs) into calls to play the role of "anxiety-inducer," freeing up the seller to focus energy on maintaining the relationship.

How to Create Anxiety Questions

Anxiety questions are powerful—but only if they are backed by relevant research, crafted carefully to maintain rapport, and delivered at the right time. Let's look at how to create your own.

Research   Since the overarching goal is to remind the prospect of the negative consequences of not acting, you'll need to identify those consequences to start. In the earlier example with the network security company, the hypothetical rep had done his research. He'd identified a similar company with similar processes and issues that had chosen not to upgrade its systems—and the outcome wasn't pretty for about 4.2 million reasons.

Question Structure   To open an unexpected dialogue that creates space for reshaping the prospect's point of view, keep things simple. Your questions should follow naturally from the contextualizing statement that demonstrates your credibility and industry knowledge. It should be quick, casual, open-ended, and invite further conversation.

Timing   This is the hard part—you'll need to ask the question, then pause. Expect the brief silence and resist the urge to jump back in immediately. Remember: If your question is truly effective, it's causing potential buyers to consider new elements that they've overlooked—give them time to digest.

Follow-up   Once buyers do re-engage, immediately transition to the positive. You might steer the conversation back toward your offerings and how you and your organization have solved similar issues in the past, or you might dig deeper into that newly surfaced business issue in hopes of expanding the need for your products/solutions. At the end of the day, it's all about propelling the conversation forward, into the future where value is realized.

Sidestepping Common Pitfalls

Questions are one of the most misunderstood aspects of selling. Every salesperson thinks they ask excellent questions, and many do. However, to truly uncover the information you need, you must be purposeful in your questioning—that starts with avoiding the most common mistakes.

The Wrong Questions   I hear the following refrain at least once a month: *We already ask questions, lots of them—look, we have a list.*

Inevitably, that list is a mile long and overwhelmingly focused on situational questions. For instance, a few years back, I was working with a company in San Diego selling a remote patient-monitoring system to hospitals. The CEO had brought my company in because he was convinced the sales organization needed a methodology to help them have better business conversations—the vice president of sales was less convinced of this fact. After all, he had his list of questions that he'd given to his sellers to discover all the information they needed to qualify the opportunity. The only problem was it read like an interrogation manual: *What's your ICU capacity? How many ventilators do you have? How many nurses are on during the day shift? How many at night? And on and on.* None of the questions fit into the solution bucket—there was no mechanism sales professionals could use to uncover the business challenges and priorities of the hospital itself. Without intel as to how their solution would connect to these larger goals, they were consistently positioned as a "nice to have."

Being Afraid to Hear "No" Open-ended questions are powerful—they're also comfortable. We routinely use them in casual social conversations, and even when we do use them in higher-stakes conversations, we know the outcome: an expansive answer. Sure, we may not get the exact information we were hunting for on round one, but no harm, no foul. You can always go at it from another angle—to a degree, everyone likes talking about themselves and their opinions.

However, if we never took it to the next level, we'd be guilty of wasting the prospect's time since it's unlikely we'd ever get to the heart of the matter. That's where probing questions come into play, and that's where you're offering two—and only two— choices: *yes or no.* In this situation, a "no" is a valid and helpful response if you take it in stride. Going back to our earlier example about the sales coaching software, if you ask, *Is that because there's no standardized structure for coaching conversations and reports?* and the prospect says, *No,* then you have two choices. First, you could open the dialogue back up by asking, *Oh, that's interesting. What do you think the problem is?* Or you might try another probing question and say, *Okay, well, do you think your sales managers are focusing on developing the right behaviors during their coaching sessions?*

The overarching principle is flexibility. O-P-C questions facilitate a natural conversation about the prospect's point of view by circling back and forth between the three question types, enabling you to develop a complete understanding of the prospect's needs, purchasing criteria, and view of the ideal solution. In turn, this understanding empowers you to set the value of your product/solution on a firm foundation by quantifying exactly how much time, money, or resources you'll save buyers—and securing their agreement on the plan for implementation.

Discovery Isn't Dead—It's Mutual   There's been an ongoing debate raging for the past few years around sales discovery. On the one hand, you have those who think buyers hate discovery and view it as a roadblock to the demos and nuanced answers they crave from vendors. On the other, you have those who view it as an essential part of the buying process. This is where I sit. I've always found that asking thought-provoking, intentional questions is not annoying—it's engaging. And it's the critical component that allows you to make the leap from seller to valued business advisor.

In an attempt to reconcile these two viewpoints, I dug deeper and found that some buyers do hate discovery—but that's only when we, as sales professionals, get it wrong. By following two guiding principles, you can ensure your discovery process is not only engaging but mutually beneficial.

1. It's Not About You   Too many sellers make the mistake of viewing discovery as a one-time event. As a result, it takes on a transactional light: *Give me this info, then I'll give you what you really want.* Sellers show up to the call equipped with a list of situational questions and attempt to run through the whole thing—exactly like the health care client in the earlier example: *What's your ICU capacity? How many ventilators do you have? How many nurses are on during the day shift? How many at night? And on and on.*

This is not a conversation—it's an interrogation. And buyers respond accordingly by putting up their guard. If that's how you run discovery, ask yourself: *Have you given them a reason to answer?* No—this is a completely one-sided event, a qualification hurdle that you're making the buyer jump that only benefits the sales organization.

By contrast, when you come prepared with insightful questions based on your research and lessons learned from other customers, you create the environment for mutually beneficial conversations. Instead of focusing on qualification questions, you're questioning process invites the prospect to articulate, examine, and potentially alter their thinking. The discovery conversation can't all be questions, either. You need to come prepared with value-added information, whether that's third-party insights into industry trends, more information on your product/services, or a customized demo.

2. Quality Over Quantity There's no magic number of questions or the perfect sales-call script out there. If you go down this path of thinking, you'll fall into the trap of overanalyzing and miss the X-factor that will make your discovery calls valuable for you and your buyer: You need to ask questions that get the prospect talking:

- After analyzing nearly one million sales calls, Chorus.ai found that "high-performing reps ask fewer questions per minute than lower-performing reps, but are able to get the prospect to open up more."[2]
- Gong.io discovered a correlation between longer prospect responses and sales success rates—and that asking too many questions actually decreases your win rate.[3]

I've seen this play out time and time again. A handful of insightful open-ended questions is all you need to get a C-suite executive talking—in fact, I've had several calls recently where executives chose to extend the time they'd scheduled for our conversation because they found it so valuable. And guess what? I asked less than 10 questions on all of those calls.

When you show up with a commitment to uncovering a potential buyer's most critical business issues and helping to solve them, sales discovery calls will always expand perspectives and add value. The trick is to remember that discovery is an ongoing process that can be used throughout the buying cycle and that it must be mutual—the salesperson needs to understand the prospect, and the prospect also needs vital information from the seller.

Every rep secretly wants to tell the buyer what to do, but when you switch your mindset from checking a box to having consultative business conversations, you improve your chances of uncovering challenges that your solution is uniquely qualified to solve. In doing so, you'll forge trusted business relationships and uncover the value that motivates action.

Create Sales Opportunities You Can Win

7

Earn Time on Their Calendar

A re you wearing a smartwatch or other fitness tracker? Good. Now take an honest look at your pipeline—what happens to your heart rate?

If it's beating in time to the tempo of your favorite pop song, you're in good company! In our recent study, "The Three Keys to Sales Quota Attainment," we found that 69% of salespeople do not have enough opportunities in their pipeline to achieve their quota. It makes perfect sense, no one likes to prospect, and odds are you've got an inconsistent approach that fails to fill the revenue pipeline.

The good news is that there's a proven method for setting more meetings and adding more qualified opportunities. The bad news is there's no silver bullet—and that's the mistake that everyone from early-career sales development representatives (SDRs) to seasoned account executives make.

At a high level, we all know how to prospect more effectively— the right message, at the right time, to the right person—and the commitment to consistently putting in the work, day in and day out. Yet, we're inevitably tempted to find that one hack that promises to make this all easy and predictable—we search for that silver bullet to take down the werewolf that is prospecting drudgery. We fall into the trap of thinking, *If only I had a better email template or a phone script to rule all phone scripts! Maybe a dialer is the only thing I'm missing? What if enablement wrote new cadences for all of our "big rock" content?*

Don't get me wrong—you'll likely see a marginal lift from all of the above. And it will be just that, *marginal.* If you want to transform your prospecting results, you must take small tweaks like the previous examples and apply them to a proven framework. After all, it's a confusing and noisy world out there. Our prospects are all bombarded with notifications and requests for their time daily, and most buyers don't think they need our products and services. By using a strategically choreographed, multichannel approach, you break through that cacophony of outreach to increase activity and conversions. Moreover, by following the approach I'll outline in this chapter, you'll not only have more wins, but you'll also learn more from every miss.

Mindset

Before we get into the specifics, I owe you a note on mindset. Make no mistake—your mindset or the mindset of your sales team is the single most important variable in this whole equation.

Nothing will have a greater impact on your success than the attitudes you hold toward yourself, your prospects, and the activity of prospecting. Think about it—you can instantly hear fear and frustration in someone's voice or pick up on body language that conveys avoidance. Yes, prospecting is *tough*; it's a slog; it's frustrating and time-consuming. And without it, you have no opportunities, no sales, and no commission checks. Before beginning outreach, always monitor three things:

1. **Focus:** Block off nonnegotiable time on your calendar, and stick to it! After all, if you don't respect your time, why should others?

2. **Confidence:** Are you confident that you're prepared to add value at every opportunity? If you don't believe it, don't expect your prospects to.

3. **Mindfulness:** What unconscious signals is your voice or body language giving off? Physicality matters—ensure you're in an energizing position, and never forget to smile, even when the prospect can't see your face.

Strategically Crafted, Multichannel Cadences

If you've done the research, you'll know a good deal about your prospects before beginning outreach. You'll have insight into their industry, their company's market position and financials, their role, and you'll have a solid understanding of likely business challenges on their radar. What you do not, and cannot, know is their preferred communication method. This is your first hurdle to clear. The second is familiarity—the prospect does not know you. Why would they spend their valuable time in a meeting?

The proven ValueSelling approach is built on a strategic, multichannel framework you'll use to overcome these challenges. At its core, it's based on the mere-exposure effect: the psychological phenomenon responsible for converting familiarity into preference. Basically, you start to prefer something merely because it's familiar to you, a known entity. This helps you build familiarity and eventually break through the noise. Now, this doesn't mean you'll send out five emails in a week and call three times the following Tuesday—this is a strategic approach that mixes communication channels and creates a whirlwind of value-added activity that's difficult to ignore. Of course, cadences alone are nothing without the messaging that powers them, so I'll also cover how to leverage the anxiety, influence, and motivation (A-I-M) framework to develop consistent messaging across channels that piques interest and creates urgency. Let's look at how this breaks down.

Vortex Sphere of Influence™

As the sales professional, you're the face of your company to your customers. However, nothing happens in a vacuum. You can leverage all the ways in which your company impacts the market, increases awareness, and provides assets to influence potential buyers. This ecosystem of interactions and content is what we call the Vortex Sphere of Influence (Figure 7.1), and it's a tremendous resource that's likely already been created for you, a wealth of tools to save you time in your goal to educate, provide insight, and learn about a prospect's unique business issues. Look on your company's website, familiarize yourself with the materials in your sales enablement platform, and reach out to marketing for intel about planned initiatives. And this sphere of influence doesn't stop with your company's materials. You can also leverage related, third-party content to increase your credibility in the prospect's mind.

Vortex Sphere of Engagement™

The Vortex Sphere of Engagement (Figure 7.2) includes all of the channels and methods you'll use to increase familiarity, educate and add value to create opportunities, and engage with potential buyers. This sphere of activity is powered by your company's Vortex Sphere of Influence, and each sphere will be unique to your goals and approach. By understanding how to leverage both in your outreach you'll accomplish the following:

- Increase engagement with prospects through respectful persistence.
- Use a cadence-based approach of value-based interruptions.
- Develop compelling messaging with the A-I-M framework.
- Leverage both your company and personal brand to connect.
- Discuss problems that you are uniquely positioned to solve.

Figure 7.1 Vortex Sphere of Influence™.
Source: Adapted from ValueSelling Associates.

The Spheres of Influence and Engagement come together to influence prospects through the multichannel cadences you'll build. A cadence is merely a series of communication outreaches

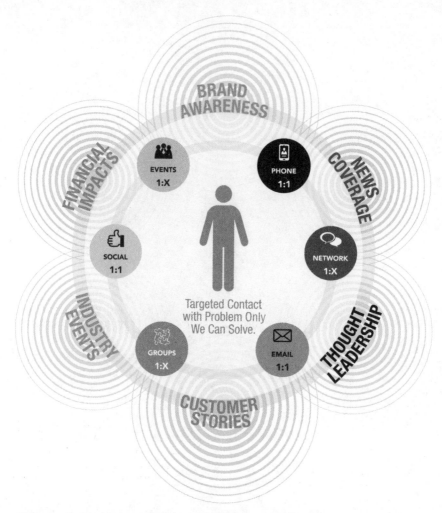

Figure 7.2 Vortex Sphere of Engagement™.

Source: ValueSelling Associates, https://www.slideshare.net/
ValueSellingAssociates/creating-a-cadence-for-topoffunnel-growth/
(last accessed April 24, 2023).

that are planned over a period. It typically takes 15–17 touches
across 20–24 business days to connect with a prospect, and by
strategically using email, video, phone calls, texts, social actions,
voicemails, and sometimes even snail mail, you'll increase
familiarity and add value without becoming a pest.

It's not all about the cadence or the volume of activity though. To build trust and credibility, you'll need to add value with every interaction.

Becoming a Value-added Interruption

As we covered in Chapter 4, no one wants to be sold to; however, people do search out trusted business advisors to help them efficiently navigate the buying journey and buy what they need. The main goal of prospecting is to establish credibility, trust, and rapport—that's what leads to a meeting and sets the groundwork for a long-lasting business relationship. To do that, you'll need to provide valuable information and insight.

What's the most valuable information you can share? All we can do is make educated guesses based on our research, interactions with similar potential buyers, and understanding of the prospect's likely business challenges. High-quality research is the foundation for everything and the most effective tool you have at your disposal to reduce the risk of approaching someone in the wrong manner. Beyond that, it's important to ensure the content and resources you share are relevant to the prospect and their challenges. Value is always determined in the mind of the buyer— it's our job to uncover what they find truly valuable and connect to that in each interaction. But first, you'll need to get their attention.

The A-I-M Framework

The A-I-M framework is a powerful template to develop messaging based on a well-researched and proven approach to increase engagement with prospects based on leveraging the way our brains react to certain situations. It breaks down like this:

- **Anxiety:** Creating anxiety triggers the "curiosity mechanism" in the brain, which strives to find a solution or understanding.

- **Influence:** Once you've piqued their curiosity, move it in the right direction by speaking to the value you've brought other customers in the past.
- **Motivation:** Circle back to the problem you can solve that provides enough value to inspire motivation and action.

For instance, maybe you're targeting a chief information officer (CIO) and reaching out via InMail or voicemail—your message might look something like this:

This is Julie at SkyLabs.

We've been working with CIOs to help them deal with major concerns like data breaches, like the one that impacted [COMPANY FROM RESEARCH] last fall. (ANXIETY)

I've helped my customers shore up network vulnerabilities that could have resulted in multimillion dollar settlements and would welcome an opportunity to discuss some approaches with you. (INFLUENCE)

I'll send a follow-up email with my contact information and look forward to speaking with you soon about how we might be able to help with your challenges. (MOTIVATION)

What makes this template so potent is its universality. It's universally applicable because it's not about you or your product—it's firmly focused on the prospect's likely business issues. This is the template you'll use throughout your cadences. Of course, you'll modify according to communication channels and customize to prospects. And you'll focus more on different elements at different stages of your cadences, but the underlying architecture will not change.

Determining the Ideal Volume

Before you can create a prospecting cadence that drives sustainable revenue gains, you'll need to know how much activity is needed. How many prospects do you actually need to achieve or overachieve your goal. Shockingly, next to no one does this—and when people do, it's treated as a once-a-year event. In reality, you need to continually monitor and refine your approach based on the current market conditions, not the conditions 12 months ago. This isn't merely about generating enough opportunities to achieve your quota; it's about how much *you* want to earn.

Once you've identified this number, work backward. To hit your target, how many deals do you need based on your average deal size? What's your average win rate? Based on win rate, calculate how many qualified prospects you need. Finally, what's your lead-to-meeting ratio? Once you've worked that out, you can estimate the number of hours you'll need to hit your goal. For example, if you need to sell $2 million to hit your goal this year, it might break down as shown in Figure 7.3.

UNDERSTAND

- How much activity is actually needed
- Your prospecting ratios

Target	2,000,000
Average Transaction Size	125,000
Total Number of Transactions Required	2m/125K = 16
Average Win Ratio (Meeting to Close)	1 out of 3
Total Qualified Prospects Required	3 x 16 = 48
Pipeline Ratio (Qualified Lead to Meeting)	1 out of 5
Total Prospecting Year – Month – Day	5 x 48 = 240 per year **or** 20 per month **or** approximately 1 per day

Figure 7.3 Calculating the Ideal Prospecting Volume.
Source: ValueSelling Associates, https://www.valueselling.com/ powerful-sales-prospecting/ (last accessed April 24, 2023).

When formulating this plan, always err on the side of caution. If your average win rate falls between one in three and one in four, plan on closing one out of every four opportunities—your pipeline will thank you later. Remember: You're not targeting anyone and everyone. As I'll discuss in detail in Chapter 8, continually qualifying prospects ensures you don't waste time chasing unwinnable opportunities and find yourself nearing the end of the quarter with a false sense of security.

Constructing Prospecting Cadences

Sales cadences are the conductor of your outreach—they'll determine which types of messages go out when and across which platforms. Like so many things in sales, effective cadences begin with research and value. The ideal cadence will vary based on the prospect's industry and role, and the first few touches should always be heavy on value and insight. If you're targeting the chief marketing officer (CMO) of a tech company, you'll want to start with LinkedIn. On the other hand, if you're going after manufacturing executives, then picking up the phone is likely the way to start.

Remember to always provide value from the very beginning. If you're trying to connect with that CMO and you start with LinkedIn, aim to engage and expand her thinking. This might take the form of reading what she is sharing and leaving an insightful, well-researched comment and sharing a resource of your own. Three days later, you might follow up with an InMail message and another resource. Then, you might add her to a call list or send an email using the A-I-M framework. Again, it might look like this:

Mary,

I found the Forrester report you shared intriguing. This report from McKinsey provides even more critical insight into the challenges executives face in capturing revenue in the competitive aviation market.

We've worked with other aviation executives like you to take advantage of these market conditions. Are you open to scheduling a 15-minute meeting so that I can provide additional information to inform your thinking?

From there, your next move might be to send another social message that shows how you've provided impactful value to similar prospects and companies in the past—followed up with another call heavy on anxiety and motivation. The key is consistency. Never go more than 5 business days between touches—this will ensure that you'll stay top-of-mind and significantly increase your odds of connecting. This sample cadence gives you an idea of how to switch between communication channels while emphasizing different elements of the A-I-M framework (Figure 7.4).

A note on LinkedIn and social selling in general: We'll discuss social selling in detail later in the chapter, I want to call out a crucial point right now. Notice that the first few social actions in the previous

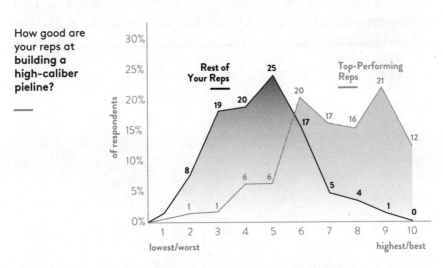

Figure 7.4 Vortex Prospecting™ Simple Cadence Construction.

Source: Adapted from ValueSelling Associates.

example did not ask for a meeting. Everyone, myself included, is sick of accepting a connection request and immediately getting hit with a pitch message and a link to schedule a meeting. Social is just that, social—it's a tool to build and expand relationships.

Once you've identified the makeup of a likely buying group, you can use the same tactics to target key individuals simultaneously. It's best practice to start by targeting three to six individuals in the same organization—to get started, look at your most common buying roles and include those in your account-based cadences. In the example in Figure 7.5, you'll see that the CEO, CFO, chief technology officer (CTO), and vice presidents (VPs) are on three different cadences that use different schedules and mixes of communication channels. And because their roles are different, the value-added content provided is different—it's highly likely that the CFO and CTO have different points of view on what is valuable.

Since you're essentially making an informed guess about a potential buyer's challenges, the content of your cadences can also vary over time. In the example in Figure 7.6, you'll see that the messaging mentions four problems over the course of 23 days. All problems are relevant to the role and the industry.

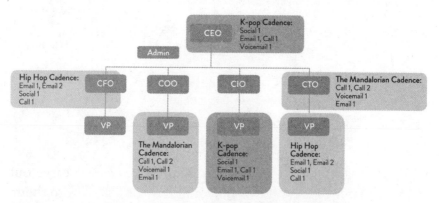

Figure 7.5 Building Account-Based Sales Cadences.

Source: ValueSelling Associates, https://www.slideshare.net/ValueSellingAssociates/creating-a-prospecting-cadence-to-drive-topoffunnel-revenue/ (last accessed April 24, 2023).

NAME: CONTACT/ROLE:
TYPE: DURATION:

PROBLEM FOCUS: **TOO MANY TECH SOLUTIONS CREATING CONFUSION**

Day 1 3rd Party	Day 2 3rd Party	Day 3 Anxiety	Day 4 Influence	Day 5 Motivation
Call 1 Email 1	Call 2 VM 1 Email 1	Call 3 Email 3	Snail Mail 1 Call 4	Call 5 Email 4

PROBLEM FOCUS: **SILO'D ORGANIZATION CREATING FRICTION, DECREASING CUSTOMER RETENTION**

Day 6 3rd Party	Day 7 Influence	Day 8 Influence	Day 9 Motivation	Day 10 Motivation	Day 11 Influence
Call 6 VM 2 Email 5	Call 7 VM 3 Email 6	Call 8 VM 4 Email 7	Snail Mail 2 Call 9 Email 8	Call 10 Email 9	Call 11 VM 5 Email 10

PROBLEM FOCUS: **DECREASE IN BRICK & MORTAR REVENUE, FRACTURED EXPERIENCE**

Day 12 Anxiety	Day 13 Influence	Day 14 Anxiety	Day 15 Influence	Day 16 Motivation	Day 17 Motivation
Call 12 Email 11	Call 13 Email 12 Snail Mail 3	Call 14 VM 6 Email 13	Call 15 VM 7 Email 14	Call 16 Email 15	Call 17 Email 16 Snail Mail 4

PROBLEM FOCUS: **CUSTOMER RETENTION DECREASING, IMPACTING REVENUE**

Day 18 3rd Party	Day 19 3rd Party	Day 20 Anxiety	Day 21 Influence	Day 22 Motivation	Day 23 Motivation
Call 18 Call 19 Email 17	Call 20 VM 8 Email 18	Call 21 VM9 Email 19	Call 22 VM 10 Email 20	Call 23 VM 11 Email 21	Call 24 VM 12 Email 22

Figure 7.6 Full Sample Sales Cadences.

Source: Adapted from ValueSelling Associates.

Blocking Time

As I touched on in the mindset section, you'll need to carve out nonnegotiable blocks of time on your calendar and stick to them. If you're planning to hit the phone hard between 10 a.m. and 12 p.m. on Tuesday mornings, commit to it. Don't skip on time allotment either. Our "B2B Prospecting Challenges from the

Front Lines" study revealed that only 18% of salespeople spend 9 hours or more prospecting weekly—aim for 2 hours daily or 10 per week to develop a pipeline that leads to quota attainment.

Of course, even though fire drills, customer needs, and last-minute requests from management will inevitably come up, never cancel your prospecting time—move that block of time to later in the day.

Tools to Help You Track Your Progress

Before we dive into the sales tech that will help you automate and accelerate parts of this process, remember the cautionary tale from Chapter 1 where the sales team sent 256,000 emails over the course of a quarter and failed to secure one meeting. Use the tech to make this outreach more targeted, more human—not to merely increase the volume or speed or your cadences. Following are the three types of tech that will deliver the most value.

1. **Identification and Research**

    These are the tools that will help you compile lists of individuals who are likely in a buying window and have a high potential to become qualified prospects. These typically work off a set of criteria based on inputs like industry, revenue, team size, etc., to provide a longer list of possible opportunities. While these tools are tremendous time savers, it's up to you to personally vet these contacts to ensure these are high-potential prospects.

    Popular examples include LinkedIn Deep Sales, Clearbit, Datanyze, DiscoverORG, and ZoomInfo.

2. **Outreach Automation**

    From tools that leverage LinkedIn events to automate outreach to email sequencers to automatic dialers, sales engagement tech aims to automate tasks, scale efforts, and provide insight into what tactics convert sales prospects into buyers. Popular examples include SalesLoft, Outreach.io, and Reply.io.

3. **Conversational Intelligence**

These AI-driven tools track and analyze your recorded sales calls. Tracking can be set up inside these systems to monitor for certain terms/phrases or leading indicators like the number and types of questions salespeople ask. Popular examples include Chorus.ai, Gong.io, and Uniphore.

If leveraged correctly, your tech stack will enable you to scale your efforts while maintaining that personalized approach that is so crucial to creating customers for life. Use these tools to track your outreach, and let the data tell you what works and what doesn't. For instance, outreach automation like SalesLoft allows you to easily test variants in your cadences and automatically selects the more effective ones. At the very least, you can always track efforts using a spreadsheet and do the analysis yourself.

Picking Up the Phone

If you're afraid to pick up the phone, you're not alone. Our "B2B Prospecting Challenges from the Front Lines" study revealed that 53% of sellers give up too easily—and 48% are afraid to start dialing in the first place. Yes, cold calling can be stressful. Let's face it: It's hard to be rejected—with varying degrees of grace—day after day. And you know what? *It works.*

After following the playbook I outline in this section, one of our client's sales teams conservatively created about $6.5M (USD) in pipeline in their first 3 days of call blocks alone. Teams weren't working the phones all day either. I'm talking about three, 60-minute call blocks where nothing happened but dialing and talking. In those 180 minutes, they created more potential pipeline than they had the entire previous quarter through email outreach alone. Perhaps it's most striking that this is the same group that told one of our associates on day one that "no one answers the phone anymore." It goes to show you that the phone is still a powerful communication tool and that when you use the phone, you will create engagement. The sellers who do not use it are proven wrong again and again.

Never underestimate the power of getting someone into a conversation.

Again, mindset is the crucial factor. Before you can realize results like this, you'll have to change your thinking. Starting today, I want you to view the phone as a critical tool for reaching prospects and providing value, not as a symbol of fear. Remember: Cold calls are a strategic interruption focused on the goal of getting a meeting or information—and even negative experiences can provide you with crucial data to help scale your success. When you do finish a tough call, take Ted Lasso's advice: *Be a goldfish*. Forget the experience, remember the lesson. With that out of the way, let's dive into how you'll build a high-caliber pipeline over the phone.

Crafting Call and Voicemail Scripts

Effective sales calls are always focused on the potential buyers and their challenges—that means coming prepared with relevant insights and information. You'll also need to capture their attention, pique interest, and be ready for the inevitable standard objections once you transition to the ask for a meeting: *I have no time. I have no need. I have no money*. And guess what? Neither of the top three is valid for a first conversation—keep digging. In addition to leveraging the A-I-M framework, you should also be prepared with a value-based story to establish credibility—and open and probing questions, as we discussed in the previous chapter, in the event that there's an opportunity to take the conversation further than expected.

If you don't know where to start with templates for your sales prospecting calls, start with the "pace/pace/lead" technique. Its power comes from the pattern interrupt—you acknowledge the situation in the first two statements by stating self-evident truths that are normally not acknowledged in most sales calls, e.g., *You don't know me (1), and you weren't expecting my call (2)*. Then you transition to a share or ask—and because the prospect agreed with the first two statements they are statistically much more likely to agree with the third. You might say something like this:

Hello, Connor. My name is Julie with ValueSelling Associates. You do not know me and were not expecting my call. The reason for my call is to see if you are available next Tuesday or Wednesday to understand more about your challenges around sales activity and possibly share how other customers have overcome these challenges with us.

Now at this point, you might be hit with an objection like, *Wait, who are you?* That's okay; it's the perfect opportunity to go into a credibility introduction like the one that follows. Of course, this is merely an example—an outline of how you'd like the conversation to go. The problem with scripts is that prospects never remembers their lines. You always need to be flexible, listen, then think, and respond.

[NAME], we work with executives like you in the [ENTER INDUSTRY NAME] industry and have helped them solve this challenge as well as others including:

- *[INDUSTRY-SPECIFIC CHALLENGE]*
- *[INDUSTRY-SPECIFIC CHALLENGE]*
- *[INDUSTRY-SPECIFIC CHALLENGE]*

Are these challenges you are currently wrestling with?

PROSPECT ANSWERS YES—Keep going

PROSPECT ANSWERS NO—What are your largest business challenges today?

[NAME], our customers include [Three INDUSTRY RELEVANT CLIENT NAMES], and in working with them we've seen:

- *[INDUSTRY-SPECIFIC RESULT]*
- *[INDUSTRY-SPECIFIC RESULT]*
- *[INDUSTRY-SPECIFIC RESULT]*

We may not be a fit for your company now, but I'd like to schedule 15 minutes when I haven't caught you off guard to discuss your challenges in more detail. I have time [ENTER DAY] and [ENTER TIME]. If that works for you, I will send a meeting invite to [CONFIRM EMAIL ADDRESS].

PROSPECT ANSWERS: No, that doesn't work for me.

YOU RESPOND: I have my calendar up in front of me, what day and time works best for you?

For voicemails, the process is similar but truncated. Strive to use the A-I-M framework, and ensure the total voicemail is no longer than 20 seconds. In general, when writing call and voicemail scripts remember to be relevant and succinct. Clear messaging wins out these days since most people tend to read their voicemails rather than listen to them. To ensure you're getting across the most valuable information in the least amount of time, write your script out, and once you're happy with it, write it again using half the words you used before. A sample voicemail script would look like this:

Connor,

This is Julie, with ValueSelling Associates

We've been working with CROs like yourself to help them deal with major concerns such as getting SDRs to set more appointments.

Connor, I've helped my customers grow their pipeline by 3x and would like an opportunity to discuss some of your issues around top-of-the-funnel activity.

I'll send a follow-up email tomorrow and look forward to speaking with you soon.

Notice that you don't ask for a callback in this example. The whole point is to prime the memory and establish credibility.

One final note: Don't forget to practice, practice . . . then practice some more, especially when it comes to responding to common objections like *I'm heading into a meeting, I have another call,* or *Now's not a good time.* And be prepared! After 10 dials and no answers, it's easy to zone out, but when they do actually pick up, you have to be ready to talk. After all, if you're unsure what to say next, it's hard to stay confident.

Call Blocks

These should be *nonnegotiable.* In the same way that I blocked out dedicated time on my calendar each week when writing this book, you must do the same for prospecting and call blocks in particular. Remember: Consistency always wins out over intensity. It's best to commit to 60 minutes of uninterrupted activity at a time. Now, that doesn't mean the first 25 minutes are spent curating your call list. Before you hit that 60-minute timer on your phone, you'll need to have your list complete, vetted for accuracy, and checked against your system of record—plus you'll need to ensure you have your introductory statements and value-based stories crafted and have valuable insights and information to share. This means that you've already set aside and completed other time blocks on things like research.

Quick win: At a bare minimum, research should involve 10 minutes on the industry, 10 minutes on the company, and 10 minutes on the prospect. Once your industry expertise increases, you can cut down the industry component to a quicker scan of the latest updates.

Okay, you're ready to start dialing; before you do, check your mindset. Many sellers make the mistake of unconsciously carrying negative emotions into their cold calling—and while you may not be able to hear the difference in your voice, the prospect certainly can. After all, most of the time we react more to *how* people say something rather than *what* they actually say.

To ensure you come off as the capable professional you are, sit or stand up straight to embody confidence, smile to improve your mood, and shut down all apps that could distract you, like Slack and email notifications. Now, this might seem like simple advice—and the impact that this simple advice has on your tone of voice can be profound.

You're probably wondering: *Julie, how many of these call blocks do I need each week?* That's an equation you'll have to figure out for yourself, which is why it's vital to track your activity by recording the following:

- Number of dials
- Number of human connections
- Number of meetings set
- Number of executive-level connections made

As we talked about earlier, the rule of thumb is that you should be prospecting at least 10 hours a week across a variety of channels. To identify the ideal number of call blocks, track the listed data for a few weeks until you can establish a baseline—then cross reference these results against the original prospecting calculation you did in the previous section. This will give you an idea of how to split your time strategically across communication channels. In addition to stats like your call-to-meeting ratio, you should also be looking for patterns in the qualitative data: Were there common objections? Did you have more success with a particular role, industry, or company size? Did your credibility introduction resonate and with whom? What did you find most challenging?

Ultimately, you need the amount of time and activity required to satisfy your goal. Negotiate what this looks like based on your role with your manager. Most salespeople have to walk the tightrope between managing the pipeline and filling it—ensure that your expectations are aligned with your manager's and allow for success in both.

Social Selling

In Chapter 4, I outlined the bare minimum you need to appear as a credible professional. Now, it's time to take a second look at your LinkedIn practices from a prospecting perspective to take things to the next level.

A High-performing Profile

As you'll also remember from Chapter 4, not all LinkedIn profiles are alike. In a March 2022 article from LinkedIn's Paul Petrone,[1] he wrote about a study that found that salespeople's profiles are viewed at twice the rate of other professionals', and prospects are 87% more likely to accept your InMail if you have a complete and professional profile.

Let's assume you've already taken care of those essentials; the next step is revisiting your headline with a value-selling mindset. Is it merely your job title, or is it an attention-grabbing statement about the value you bring to clients? This might feel like semantics, but when you're targeting an executive who's bombarded with requests for connecting, having a headline that stands apart from the slew of headshots and headlines in the pending invitations section is a tremendous advantage.

From here, assess your "About" and "Experience" sections. Your "About" section should present you as authentic, professional, and personable. Here's the area to talk about why you choose to do what you do and work where you work—it's also an ideal place to include a credibility introduction. Yes, be professional here, but also be human—ditch the third-person perspective and industry jargon to share an approachable version of your expertise. *Hint: focus on the value you bring your customers.* The "Experience" section should follow suit—explain in clear language the overview of your role *and* the goals you accomplished in those roles. If you have materials that offer a more detailed description of these experiences, be sure to put those in the

"Featured" section. You can also leverage your company's sphere of influence here—focus on compelling resources like ebooks and videos that speak to the types of buyers you're targeting.

How many groups have you joined? How many do you manage? Groups are an effective prospecting aid as they enable you to send messages to other group members without being connected—and you can join up to 100 and manage up to 20. I'd recommend joining a mix of groups. The groups dedicated to helping sales professionals sell better are a fantastic arena for professional development and increasing your thought leadership within the community. From a prospecting perspective, begin with the groups where your target buyers are and where they are most active. Now, don't treat these like a leads list and send InMails to anyone and everyone in the latest CTO group. At first, you'll want to engage earnestly in the group discussions and share readily—that way you'll already have a foundation of credibility to accompany your first InMail.

How's that "Recommendations" section looking? It's tempting to overlook this profile section or dismiss it as merely a tool used by job seekers—and it's vital to establish your credibility. Uplift your network by giving recommendations to colleagues and clients, and don't be shy about asking for them either. One effective and underutilized tactic is to give unsolicited recommendations to clients. Not only does this help to strengthen your relationship, but if they choose to approve it and add it to their profile, you'll have a near-permanent foothold that essentially acts as a standing advertisement for your credibility. Here again, the overarching principle is *give freely*.

Speaking of your network, how extensive is it? These days, having 500+ connections feels like table stakes, and the bigger your network, the more likely it is that your next prospect will be a second-degree connection. Focus on connecting with a few high-profile influencers in the right industries to speed up the process and expand your ability to connect with more individuals.

Don't be secretive about these activities either. As I mentioned earlier, LinkedIn found that potential buyers were 86% more likely to accept your InMail if they noticed you viewed their profile first. Navigate to the "Settings & Privacy" section of your profile, then "Visibility," followed by "Profile viewing options," and ensure your settings show your name and headline to users when you view their profile.

Social Selling Actions

Attending industry events on LinkedIn is a fantastic way to gain insight into the challenges facing companies in this space. Pay particular attention to the Q&A section at the end—what types of questions are your target prospects asking, what terms are they using, and what themes emerge? Even if you're not able to attend the entire event, signing up for the event allows you to message other event attendees without being connected to them—a useful tool for navigating the 100-per-week guideline that LinkedIn imposed on connection requests in 2021.

Reconnecting with champions who have moved onto new jobs is another way to become more targeted in social selling. Ideally, you should already have lead and account lists set up in a tool like LinkedIn's Sales Navigator to send you alerts on company news and job changes. However, you can also target known fans of your products and services with a more general search using LinkedIn's "Past Companies" filters. For instance, if you know you've had a raving fan base at company X for the past 2 years, see who's moved on. Any buying roles in the mix? Odds are there are going to be a few who have a favorable impression of your company. All that's left to do is reach out and get the conversation going.

Once you've taken the time to elevate your personal brand on LinkedIn and establish your network, dive into outreach. Remember, the idea is to be a value-added interruption and focus on relationship building. Once you've identified the individuals who will likely be on the buying committee at a target account, see who's shared a post recently. Make a point to like and comment on their posts and note this activity in your system of record. Based on their activity, find a valuable resource to offer in return. You'll want to offer this up freely without an ask at first—then you could add this person to a call list, send another InMail or send them an email that expands on the first resource you sent, and ask for the meeting. Again, you'll follow the A-I-M framework to create urgency once you've moved past those initial interactions that are solely focused on value.

Emails That Get Opened

Strategically choreographed cadences require multiple emails across the length of the cadence, and you can switch between the components of the A-I-M framework to amplify your message. If your first email was focused on anxiety, the next email in your cadence should focus on the influence component and demonstrate that it's worth the prospect investing their precious time in you. Ultimately, the goal is to find the motivating element here—that might be anxiety or influence; it's whatever resonates with the buyer.

If you start with anxiety, that first email might look something like this:

[PROSPECT NAME],

I am sending a similar email to [COWORKER], [COWORKER], and [COWORKER] to determine who at [COMPANY NAME] would have the most interest in speaking with me about [LIKELY BUSINESS CHALLENGES].

Working with other companies and executives in your role, we have achieved [VALUE RESULTS] and [BUSINESS RESULT].

I have time [SPECIFIC DATE RANGE (e.g., Tuesday and Thursday afternoon PT)] to talk in more detail. If that doesn't work, please suggest a time that does.

If that second email focuses on influence, it will read like this:

[PROSPECT NAME],

I shared a Forrester report with you on LinkedIn and believe this one from McKinsey provides even more key insight into [LIKELY BUSINESS CHALLENGES].

We've worked with other [INDUSTRY] executives like you to take advantage of these unique market conditions, and I'd like to schedule 15 minutes to provide more information to guide your thinking.

A note on personalization: Make no mistake, your messaging should be personalized to the prospect's industry, company, role, and likely business challenges they're facing—and that's enough. With the amount of data available, some salespeople are tempted to go further to stand apart, and this can backfire. There is a point where outreach can cross the line from personalized to creepy. Everyone wants you to understand their business, but no one wants to feel that their privacy has been compromised.

Quick win: Double-check your system of record—nothing kills credibility faster than when automation goes wrong and you wind up sending out emails with subject lines that contain, "[Name]" or transpose their first and last name. I can't tell you how many emails I've gotten that start with "Dear Thomas."

Video

The king and queen of content: *video*. Don't neglect this useful tool in your cadences—inserting short videos into emails is a tremendous way to stand out and convey information succinctly. You can use video for introductions, another follow-up step in your cadence, customized demos, or to reengage prospects later on as an opportunity unfolds. With the exception of demos, keep these short—90 to 120 seconds is all you need to efficiently convey your message and include a direct call-to-action. As noted before, the A-I-M framework—particularly the influence component—is the ideal template for building out your content.

The next step is recording, and while this isn't vastly different from your typical Zoom presence, a few extra steps should be taken:

- Select a quiet location with low ambient noise and use an external or headset mic.
- Upgrade to a 1080 or 4K webcam and position it at eye level so that you can look directly into the camera.
- Choose a large, well-lit, simple environment as a background—and use an external ring light to avoid distracting shadows and camera focusing issues.
- Avoid complex patterns in clothing—they can create a moiré pattern when the video is compressed or scaled.
- Once your video is complete, create a personalized thumbnail that captures the prospect's attention at a glance.

■ ■ ■

In the end, prospecting success will always hinge on two vital components: measurement and consistency. Understanding the science behind effective sales cadences and the best practices for each channel only gets you so far. You'll need to continually measure your progress so that you can adjust and improve. In an ideal world, enablement helps you track things like the number of cadences, the number of dials, emails and social actions, and what element of your cadences and which content generates the best results. If they don't, track them yourself to have the highest level of insight into what's working and what's not. You'll also need the discipline to commit to prospecting and stick to it. Spending 25 minutes a day on the previous activities won't get you far. Aim to spend 2 hours each day on targeted outreach— that's in addition to list preparation, research, CRM updates, cadence personalization, understanding the sphere of influence, analysis, practice, and dedicated skill improvement. Only then will you have the volume of strategic activity you need to build a pipeline of winnable opportunities.

8

Uncover Business Problems Worth Solving

The idea that people need a reason to change is the most basic and obvious of concepts. Change is difficult for most people: It includes risk, uncertainty, and the likelihood that they're going to have to put in long hours and effort to successfully manage the change.

Today, more than ever, clients don't buy because they fall in love with a product. They buy because they have a need that requires a solution. They buy for their reasons, not ours.

Why did technology sales explode during the pandemic? It's simple—when employees were 100% forced to work from home, businesses had no in-home infrastructure to accommodate the new work requirements.

Companies who would not take a sales call from web conferencing, VPN (virtual private network) providers, and other technology infrastructure companies suddenly could not purchase those products fast enough. Consumers who had rarely used restaurant or grocery delivery services turned to those solutions exclusively.

Timing Is Everything

Ten years ago, our clients began asking if we could provide virtual learning options. Our answer was, "Of course!" We purchased the necessary tech, trained our team, and were ready with this new offering in under 6 months. What happened? Sure, clients explored the offerings. Yes, clients appreciated the fact that we had flexible options . . . and no, clients did not purchase the virtual option.

That all changed in March 2020. Suddenly, face-to-face and in-person training wasn't an option—and the virtual option we had provided 10 years ago was outdated; not one person on my team even remembered the experience. Even the tech I had purchased for this very purpose had long since been cancelled and deinstalled.

And yet, we had no choice. We *had* to change. We had to change *now*.

The products that we purchased were *no* different in March 2020 when I could not get them installed fast enough than they were in February 2020 when I would not even waste a nano second thinking about them.

It wasn't about the product at all. It was about my problems, my urgency, and my need. And that's the sizable problem with product-led sales: It simply isn't consultative. Product-led sales requires the customer to figure out the need—it's an approach that makes assumptions about the problems and the fact that they are worth solving.

Regardless of what you sell, you probably wouldn't be in sales if you didn't believe in your product or service. Still, the fact that you can clearly see the benefit for your customer is not enough. You cannot *force* a customer to change. You can't even *force* someone to understand things in the exact way that you understand them.

Your goal is to facilitate the customer's problem-solving experience—to arrive at the idea of your product or service by first guiding them to identify their issues and uncover the reasons they need to change. Once they see sufficient need, you can help them see why your solution is best, which will motivate them to become a client or customer of yours.

To convince a prospect that change is needed, you must be able to resolve an issue worth resolving. It doesn't matter if you have the best product or solution out there if all you have is a solution in search of a problem. Your goal in connecting to a reason to change is to connect to something that is bigger than simply solving a problem or eliminating a nuisance.

There are two clear motivators to making change:

- Business issues—business goals and objectives
- Personal issues—individual goals and objectives

Business issues are the high-level impediments to an organization achieving its goals and objectives. We use the word "business issue" because it goes beyond a salesperson's understanding of the corporate objective of the organization. The corporate objective must be difficult to achieve to create a business issue. It must be a stretch. It's something that the company cannot attain with its current way of doing things.

It is *the reason* to change.

Business issues are often the gap between current results and future results. They represent the reason organizations seek solutions—and they typically fall into three major categories:

- Revenue growth or making money
- Cost savings or keeping money
- Regulatory compliance

Going back to my example during the pandemic—I had two business issues that appeared on my radar overnight. First, our revenue model was at risk due to the global shut down. There was no way I would be able to achieve my planned business revenue results with our current business model. I had to change, or I would have gone out of business.

Second, due to government regulations, travel restrictions, mandated social distancing, and other factors around business gatherings, I was forced to reinvent our product delivery. I had to be compliant again or be put out of business for violating new government mandates, health risks, and legal implications of a face-to-face training and consulting practice.

On the other hand, personal issues have to do with the individual you are selling to. Just like a business issue, a personal issue sits between people's objectives and a gap that is preventing them from reaching their goals.

For years, I have worked with a few companies who sell luxury goods. Real luxury. For example, private jets. Their clients are celebrities in entertainment, sports, and business. They sell to the 1% of the 1%.

Turns out, if you're looking to fly privately, you have many different options. These options all have different investment levels, accounting implications, and even status associated with all of the various alternatives facing a buyer.

The personal issue that the individual may have may be status, peace of mind, safety, comfort, flexibility, or something else. One could argue that a private jet is a private jet—yet, the sales professionals I work with have sold to a higher goal or personal issue than merely the product itself. The reason to change from commercial transportation to private isn't a product decision. The decision is based on aligning to the personal issue of the individual involved in the purchase.

When you are making *big* purchases for *big* dollars, people naturally go through a more thorough evaluation and comprehensive process.

Clarifying Initiatives and Issues

There's a distinct difference between key initiatives or goals and business issues.

A business goal or objective is what customers need to accomplish to maintain or grow their business. A business issue is something customers need to address and resolve to achieve their objective, a high-level impediment, or barrier that makes that stated objective difficult to achieve or puts its achievement at risk. If the objective is simple or easy to achieve, there is no reason to change.

Once that issue is identified, drill down for a problem to solve—a difficulty that prevents your prospect from being able to satisfactorily resolve his business issue. The problem is the root cause of why that issue is difficult. Whether you are coming in with a new solution or trying to displace an existing vendor, if you can't uncover a reason for change, neither will your prospect, and nothing will happen. Once you identify the root cause, the door is open to connect your solution to the problems rolling up to that issue and demonstrate your unique value.

At times, prospects will present themselves to you who are focused on an "initiative." In the context of this discussion, an initiative is typically a "solution" that they are looking to resource and fund. I had a client recently tell me that he had an initiative to sell the breadth of the company's product line every time. The initiative was to build the skillset and mindset to expand its opportunity size in every account.

That initiative was resourced. Executive management was assigned resources and funding to ensure the goals were met. The initiative was not the issue, the initiative was the answer. As I partnered with this client, my initial job was to understand the business issue and the problems the company had already identified and diagnosed—in order to fully understand why this initative had been prescribed as the antidote.

Here's a helpful question to ask yourself when you are identifying the need to change: *Would they use my product or service if it were free?* You can have the best product available, but if customers don't understand and connect with the business and personal issues, they won't buy it—or take it even if it is free—because they don't see the value.

Connecting the Dots for Your Customers

As sales professionals, our goal is to facilitate the process a buyer would go through to buy our products and services.

Today's customers expect *you* to fit into *their* process, not the other way around. They are savvier and less dependent on suppliers for education, and they expect more in terms of linking the impact of your products and services to their business issues. Don't try to force them to come to you; you must go to them.

To do this, you have to determine what drives them, and the only way to understand this and adopt their language is by moving beyond the problems they're trying to solve and getting them to define the business and personal issues that are important. This will enable you to connect to—and ultimately demonstrate—the true value of your solution, i.e., how it will positively impact the metrics they acknowledge as key.

The process begins with a business issue discussion.

While you'll often hear from a prospect that their issue is to increase revenue or reduce expenses, those aren't issues—they are objectives. Be careful not to confuse the two. Objectives relate to goals; issues relate to the operational gap to achieve those goals. The objective may be to increase revenue; the issue is how they're going to do it.

Clarity on the business issue is vital. Why? Your next step is to identify the root cause of the issue. We call those problems.

I have never met a sales rep who didn't acknowledge that uncovering the recognized problems facing an organization is key to selling your solution.

And here is the problem with only focusing on problems.

Not all problems are worth solving. Think about it: We can't fix everything all at once. Not only is that not possible, it is not practical. The problems that get solved are the ones that are recognized to have a direct impact on reducing the risk of the business issue.

Deliberate identification of problems is incomplete. Those problems have to be worth solving if you want to be the vendor who is a necessity and not the vendor who is a nicety.

Our goal as a sales rep is to draw a straight line of acknowledgment and confirmation from the business issue to the underlying problems, and ultimately, to our solution—the best mechanism to achieve the desired outcomes.

Help prospects connect the dots; then, they can form a picture that appeals to them. You do that through deliberate conversations that reveal a shared understanding and ensure that the connection is overt and obvious in the customer's mind.

People don't like to be sold to—they like to buy, and your job is to help them, to instill confidence in that buying decision.

Asking Questions

We've already discussed the issue of trust and how salespeople were historically stereotyped as self-serving and untrustworthy because we're perceived as product pushers who do not listen or provide creative solutions.

To overcome this perception, you must evolve as a business consultant. Asking the right questions at the right times and actively listening to the answers is the fuel of the ValueSelling process.

Selling isn't merely telling—it's engaging. Prospects aren't looking for people to talk *at* them. They're seeking professionals who are interested in them, in their perspective, and who care enough to listen.

Successful salespeople know that sales isn't about pitching. It's about managing conversations; consequently, the customer comes to the same conclusions that we have, with first-hand knowledge and experience.

At the most basic level, mastering the ValueSelling Framework is about conducting better conversations with our customers and prospects—targeted and deliberate conversations that guide potential buyers through their purchasing decisions and create long-term customer relationships.

The most successful salespeople are also the most curious. They are truly interested in learning about the companies and individuals they work with. They don't conduct interrogations—they converse to learn the critical things they need to know to be successful in helping their prospects. They realize that many of us struggle to be understood: We often demonstrate more value to our customers through the questions we ask than the answers we give—we help to refine and further their thinking.

For instance, I've worked with several companies selling online learning options to primary, upper, and higher education institutions over the years. Each of these companies appeared on the scene with an extremely cool product that provided a new paradigm to augment traditional education. As they came to market, the number one goal of their sales organizations was to get the product into teacher and faculty hands—they gave it away for short demos and trials and opened every sales call with a demo. In fact, in some cases, the only product education and sales skills training provided were demo skills.

Guess what? They sold some business; they converted some trials to paid subscriptions; they steadily closed transactions. Sure, the deals were small, and they weren't exactly strategic, but that business model got many of these companies off the ground. The only problem is, it won't keep you off the ground.

When I first met the new vice president of sales at one of these organizations, he shared that his task was to put the company in a position to have a successful IPO (initial public offering). The goal was accelerated revenue; the business issue was a need to grow its transaction size and sell at the district or the institutional level, not merely to a single teacher or department.

And management had already identified a number of problems that were preventing them from addressing the business issue:

- Sales reps didn't ask the right questions.
- They didn't understand the impact of their products on a school district's success, or what criteria made a school district successful in the first place.
- They didn't engage the people who would participate in more strategic business conversations.
- They didn't listen—they demoed.

That's it—a true definition of a product-led sales process in a nutshell.

The easy business was gone—they knew they had to reinvent their approach if they wanted significantly different results, which is where we came in. Sales reps were *prohibited* from doing a demo until they understood the issue and problems a prospect was addressing. If you haven't uncovered issues and problems worth solving, don't waste your time pushing a solution.

The results were swift and significant. Their average deal size grew from approximately $5,000 to $18,000 inside of 30 days.

Being Curious

People don't care how much you know until they know how much you care.

—Theodore Roosevelt

Like most sales professionals, you're probably highly knowledgeable about the capabilities of the products and services you represent. You most likely have passion and conviction about them and are excited about discussing those capabilities and their impact. However, being a "solution expert" alone is not enough. When that's all you are, you end up trying to push products and services without really knowing whether or not your prospects actually have a need for them.

In contrast, the best sales professionals are actually problem experts. They diagnose before they prescribe. After all, if I uncover more problems than those initially disclosed, I can propose a significantly larger solution. Unfortunately, many sales reps fall into the trap of hearing one or two problems from the prospect and then immediately explaining how they have the best solution. At this point, they've stop probing for more problems altogether and move to pitching their solution.

The risk is obvious: With an incomplete diagnosis, you lose the opportunity to be uniquely qualified to satisfy the problems. You also might miss the opportunity to sell the breadth and depth of your solution.

On the other hand, that's what being a "problem expert" rather than a "solution expert" is all about. You focus the conversation on the uniqueness of your prospect as long as possible and avoid talking about your product too soon. Using this approach, you become more consultative in your sales process, and ultimately move beyond the role of vendor to the role of trusted business advisor.

When you're collaborating with your prospects, you have the opportunity to create solutions in which the prospect can take ownership prior to the actual purchase. Think about it this way: When you buy a house, the most significant purchase that many of us will make, you're not buying the concrete, lumber, drywall, and shingles. You're buying your life in that house—the neighborhood, the schools, the location, the architectural style, the family gatherings and parties, the memories to come. A successful real estate sales agent is going to find out what's important to you and what features you believe will meet your needs. Then, as you tour houses, the agent will relate these features to the life you want to have in your new home.

Most sales programs teach salespeople how to identify a prospect's problem and then explain how that problem can be solved with the salesperson's product or service: the sales pitch. Sure, that might work—but it's often insufficient for the prospect to make the decision to ultimately purchase from you instead of someone else.

The key to being a resource rather than merely a source is to uncover what they think it will take to solve the problem, find out what solutions they have tried and with what results and what they like or dislike about various approaches to the solution. When you understand the problem as well as what the prospect needs and desires in a solution, you create a better context for describing your solution. This process enables you to position what you're offering—even if it's an off-the-shelf product—as a collaborative solution. Your message is not only that you have what the prospect needs, but that you have exactly what the prospect has told you they need.

Getting into Your Prospect's Head

Your prospect's perception is the reality you need to manage. For example, have you ever been in a situation where early in the conversation a prospect tells you they know all about your company? It's possible that they do—but what if they don't? What if what they think they know is not accurate? Their perception could have a major influence on their buying decision, either in your favor or against you. They may be willing to buy something from you, but what if they're buying the wrong solution or have outrageous expectations? Those sales do more harm than good.

Salespeople often run into the trap of not knowing what their prospects do or don't understand. To be successful, it is critical to connect to and confirm that the prospect's understanding of your solution is complete and correct and to do that from the prospect's perspective and in the prospect's language. If a prospect tells you they know all about your company and offerings, ask them to tell you what they know. This will reveal how accurate their information is as well as give you insight into the problems they need to solve.

How do you get into your prospect's head? You listen.

Let's face it—listening is hard. Many of us haven't been taught to listen. Many of us have bought into the illusion that what we say is more important than what someone else says. It is a dangerous lie for sales professionals. What makes it so difficult is the fact that we're not hardwired to listen. Our brains can process information much faster than we can speak. The result is that while others speak, we're racing ahead to think about our response rather than fully engage in listening and understanding.

Listening has become even more difficult in today's world of bite-sized media and apps designed to pull our attention away at every chance. We've been conditioned to lose focus, to engage with the alert so we don't miss anything, to scroll quickly past when something doesn't immediately captivate us. These behaviors we've developed hurt us in a conversation.

To listen, we have to pay attention. Let's examine that phrase closer, "pay attention." It's explicit in the construction of the language: Attention is something we *pay* for, an act of giving something up. And according to Stephen Covey, to truly pay attention, we need to listen to understand not to respond. We need to clear distractions and be aware of our biases and predispositions.

To listen with empathy and understanding, we can't let our experience be our enemy. Even when we have heard it before, we have to listen, in the moment, to the individual who expects to be seen and heard.

Making the Connection

Alright, we've prepared for our sales call and opportunity. We've completed research on the company and the person, predicted the likely issues and problems, have secured the appointment, and are prepared to engage.

What does this preparation look like? How do you go about making the connection? It's all about creating relevant questions to uncover the prospect's point of view. Have you ever noticed that sometimes people come to the same conclusion yet communicate that conclusion in different ways? That's why we ask good questions to understand the other person's frame of reference. It helps us figure out what the prospect knows, thinks, desires, needs, and requires. We ask thoughtful and targeted questions because the questions themselves and the elegant way we conduct the conversation demonstrates our subject matter expertise.

Then, we listen to understand. We force ourselves to listen instead of merely waiting for our turn to talk. We take notes to confirm the key points we've heard and clarify our understanding—this is active listening in action. Finally, we connect the dots for the prospect. We connect their needs and their problems to our capabilities, substantiate that those problems are worth solving, and confirm the connection to the business issue, their reason to change. When we validate that they're on the same page with us, we aren't selling them anything. We are facilitating their best decision and focusing on the positive outcomes.

In the ValueSelling Framework, this process of connection is called creating a Differentiated VisionMatch™. This is a collaborative selling approach that allows you to compete on value, not price, and gets the prospect working with you, not resisting you. This process provides a unique experience to the buyer when we execute it well. Ultimately, every buyer we deal with must come to the conclusion that we are the best option for them at this point in time.

Begin at the End

The process of developing a Differentiated VisionMatch starts with a clear picture of the final result. In other words, deliberate, purposeful preparation to guide the sales call and conversation.

As a sales professional, prospects expect you to have a thorough understanding of your capabilities, the reasons your customers buy from you, and the benefits you bring to both the businesses and individuals you serve. The collaborative approach of gaining insight to the prospect's point of view adds to this equation by giving you the ability to manage the conversation and uncover the prospect's perspective. From there, you bring up conditions they may not have considered and mutually create a solution that will enable prospects to achieve their goals.

So, start with your solution—ask yourself: *What do we provide that's different from any alternative?* When you have the answer to that, the next question is: *Why would a company or individual need that capability?* Now you can shape those statements into direct questions that will help your prospect to understand and confirm in their own terminology how your product uniquely solves their business issues and problems—and satisfies the questions they must resolve in order to purchase.

For example, let's say you sell software and your company is now adding professional services.

Understanding professional services means that we know what that solution is. We could augment their staff with professionals who can take the workload and get the project completed on time.

Why would a company need that? There could be several reasons or problems that exist. Do they have enough staff? Is the staff that they do have trained in the software? Do they have implementation experience?

I would start a conversation to identify an opportunity for professional services by probing for those problems. If they exist and are acknowledged, great, have I got a solution for you. If they don't, then spending time pitching professional services is probably a terrible waste of the prospect's time.

At the end of the day, your job is not to tell prospects what their problems are. Your job is to have a conversation to identify what problems they recognize and potentially add additional problems that they might recognize based on your questions. Your job is not to destroy trust and rapport by demanding that prospects follow your rules. A sales professional's job is to manage the conversation in a way that helps prospects articulate what they think the problems are and what they think they need in order to overcome them, guiding them to a solution that only you can deliver.

9

Eliminating No-decision Opportunities and Improving Forecast Accuracy

I want you to meet Jason—he's a manager in the enterprise sales team at an analytics firm whose logo you'd instantly recognize, and he's sitting down with his vice president, Randall, to deliver his sales forecast for the second quarter. Randall looks over Jason's materials, Jason calls his attention to the key data points, and the two men discuss the finer points of a few projections. It's smiles all around, a joke or two, and the already-confident Jason leaves Randall's office feeling assured that his predictions will manifest into reality.

Now, let's go back in time to the night before this meeting. It's 9:49 p.m., and Jason's sure he's going to be the last to leave the building. Looking around his office, he's confronted with piles of data that are impossible to synthesize into a coherent picture: It's a mess of historical data, opportunities broken down by sales stage, sales cycle length, a complete pipeline analysis, lead scores, lead-gen projections, and a slew of CRM notes from sales reps that miraculously all say something like, *This one is going to close for sure!*

Exhausted, overwhelmed, and now doubting the existence of objective truths altogether, he does what he's done every time before—he goes with his gut.

Sound familiar?

Despite sales leaders' best efforts, most forecasting procedures resemble a blindfolded person throwing darts at the dartboard and seeing what sticks—and this guesswork is more widespread than you might think. According to a 2022 study by Outreach, 60% of sales leaders surveyed said they do not have a well-defined or scientific approach to forecasting.[1] This certainly fits with my experience—throughout my career, I've received the impression that most sales leaders run through forecasting activities on a mix of instinct, adrenaline, and anxiety.

It makes perfect sense—most organizations lack a common language and criteria to describe and evaluate opportunities, and most reps treat qualification as a mere stage in the sales process. So, what you wind up with is an organizational game of "telephone" where insight and information degrade at every step along their journey from account executive to chief revenue officer (CRO).

And by the way, CRM cannot solve this problem. The data in CRM exists primarily through the filter of the sales rep's data entry.

It doesn't have to be this way. Accurate and reliable forecasting has the power to transform a sales organization—and the credibility of the sales leader. It all begins with a common language for discussing opportunities and a proven framework that enables ongoing qualification. The immediate benefits come in the form of salespeople maximizing selling time and leadership making more informed decisions about go-to-market (GTM) strategy—and there's also a cultural impact that can't be overlooked. When everyone across the revenue function evaluates and discusses opportunities in the same way, you invite more perspectives and up-level skills across teams.

For example, we recently worked with a global engineering firm that regularly competes against companies five times their size. As a result, they could not afford to waste time and resources creating expensive proposals for unwinnable opportunities. The whole organization needed to rigorously qualify prospects using the same set of criteria. To accomplish this, they used the approach I'll outline in this chapter and saw transformational results, including an 833% increase in average deal size and a 40% reduction in cost of acquisition.

That's not even the impressive part—this new way of doing business has had a more profound impact on the sales culture. This shared language and approach ushered in a culture of accountability where cross-functional teams push each other toward a new standard of sales excellence. Since their proposal creation procedures involve individuals from all disciplines, e.g., sales, engineering, IT, legal, and finance, their lead review process has followed suit. Business development professionals know they will have to defend every deal they bring to the table, and other disciplines come prepared with detailed insights and challenges to examine the case from all angles. In turn, this mindset and process shift created an efficient sales force that's eager to chase new business.

A knowledge-sharing and sales-coaching perspective also provides tremendous benefits. Salespeople are competitive by nature—they can also be extremely collaborative. When you create an environment where all customer-facing roles can learn from the success and failure of others, it enables sellers to replicate best practices and leverage expertise across the sales organization with remarkable speed.

On the sales coaching side, it all comes down to understanding and expectations. When everyone uses the same language and process for qualification, you dramatically reduce the chance of errors and save both time and energy. Instead of meeting forecasting calls with anxiety and the temptation to explain every detail, salespeople know what to expect. They know exactly how their opportunities will be evaluated, which cuts the fluff and allows everyone to focus on the actions required to either move the opportunity forward or release it from their pipeline.

I've even seen these two mechanisms combine to create a de facto peer-to-peer coaching culture. One of our clients—a rapidly growing data analytics company—enabled its enterprise teams with a common language, framework, and toolset for approaching complex opportunities. Since most of its enterprise teams are made up of early-career sellers, management felt intimidated by the scope of these complex sales—the proof-of-concept period itself typically lasts 5 months. However, thanks to open knowledge-sharing and the peer-to-peer coaching culture that's sprung up around it, these valuable and complex programs now feel approachable. The result is improved sales metrics and a fundamentally changed seller experience. Instead of feeling like order takers, salespeople are empowered to have business conversations that allow them to create large-scale initiatives that transform organizations.

These are merely a few examples. The true power of this approach lies in its application across the entire revenue engine. Not only do lead conversion and sales results improve, but so does the overall customer experience (CX). Think seamless handoffs between sales and customer success, where customer success managers (CSMs) can be quickly brought up to speed on what the customer values and the agreed-upon roadmap for arriving there. If issues pop up and SMEs need to be brought in from across the organization, the same framework enables them to understand the client's business issues, problems, and goals, and to work to bring the business back on track. As humans, we seek stability and dependability. When you create a consistent CX across the entire customer life cycle, you build loyalty and create customers for life.

With this in mind, let's look at the framework you'll use to continuously qualify prospects, maximize selling time by only pursuing winnable opportunities, and improve your win rate.

The Four Questions for Efficient Qualification

As you well know, opportunities end in one of three ways: closed-won, closed-lost, or no-decision. In my experience, these outcomes are typically split evenly—you'll win roughly 33%, lose the other 33%, and in the remaining 33% of cases the prospect does nothing. And a subtle manipulation of these proportions can lead to a big payoff.

Think about what happens if you eliminate no-decision opportunities from your pipeline sooner rather than later. What impact would this have? Well, cutting the number of no-decisions in half increases your close rate from 33.3% to 40%. And converting half of those no-decisions into wins would increase your win rate to 50%. (See Figure 9.1.)

This isn't astrophysics, and it does require a consistent framework and diligent application—not surprisingly, it's

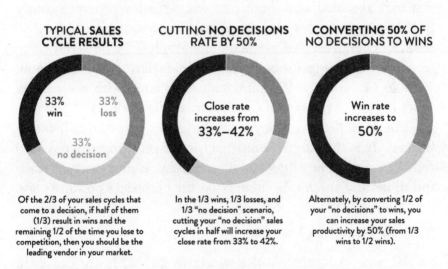

TYPICAL SALES CYCLE RESULTS

33% win — 33% loss — 33% no decision

Of the 2/3 of your sales cycles that come to a decision, if half of them (1/3) result in wins and the remaining 1/2 of the time you lose to competition, then you should be the leading vendor in your market.

CUTTING NO DECISIONS RATE BY 50%

Close rate increases from 33%–42%

In the 1/3 wins, 1/3 losses, and 1/3 "no decision" scenario, cutting your "no decision" sales cycles in half will increase your close rate from 33% to 42%.

CONVERTING 50% OF NO DECISIONS TO WINS

Win rate increases to 50%

Alternately, by converting 1/2 of your "no decisions" to wins, you can increase your sales productivity by 50% (from 1/3 wins to 1/2 wins).

Figure 9.1 The Benefits of Eliminating No-decision Opportunities.

Source: Adapted from ValueSelling Associates.

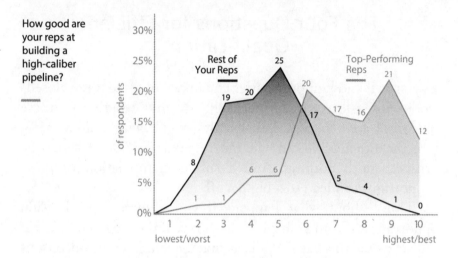

Figure 9.2 Curating a Pipeline of Qualified Opportunities

Source: Adapted from *7 Actionable Habits of Top Performers,* ValueSelling Associates, 2021.

something that high-performers figured out long ago. Our research revealed that high-performing sales reps rigorously qualify opportunities and are consistent about prospecting to build a dependable and predictable sales pipeline: When it came to "building a high-caliber pipeline," top performers scored an average of 7.3 on a 10-point scale compared with an average score of 4.5 for the rest of the reps. (See Figure 9.2.)

The trick is using a buyer-centric and rigorous qualification process. It is the single crucial factor for reducing the risk of a full, yet stalled pipeline—it all starts by asking yourself four questions and answering them from the prospect's point of view.

Should They Buy?

At the time of writing in the winter of 2022–23, my LinkedIn alerts are a steady stream of layoff notifications. While I cannot predict the future, it's one of several signals pointing toward a possible economic downturn or an economy that will keep hinting at one for the time being. In environments like this, decision-makers hide behind an additional layer of skepticism and become more risk-averse.

Plus, from our discussion in Chapter 4, it's clear that trust between B2B buyers and sellers is already strained and that trust, like credibility and rapport, must be forged on the individual level, which is why you must ask: *Should the prospect buy?* Most importantly, you must do so from *the prospect's* perspective and honestly evaluate whether your solution is a good fit. What's driving their need to change and to change now? As we talked about in the last chapter, it can only be one thing: a business issue. It's worth repeating that many sales professionals can develop a working understanding of the company's top-level business drivers, and they struggle to adequately understand the complex and cross-functional issues that get in the way of those key business objectives. From there, it's about uncovering the specific problems that make this business issue challenging to solve. Can you clearly and effectively position your product/ service as the unique solution to the specific problems that make the business issue so convoluted in the first place? If not, good luck convincing a buyer that this is the case—do yourself a favor and release this fish back into the river.

You should have answers to the following questions:

- What is the high-level business issue?
- Is this issue measurable, time bound, and related to the business objective?
- What are the problems that are getting in the way?
- Does your solution solve those problems?
- Has your prospect shared what they need?
- In the prospect's mind, is your solution the best alternative?

Is It Worth It?

Okay, let's say you checked both of the previous boxes: You know the business issue inside and out and confirmed that your solution will directly impact it. Fantastic. The next decision the buyer has to make is, *Is it really worth it?*

Every customer has to justify the purchases that they make to the business. Maybe that justification has to be reviewed by procurement or a finance professional. Maybe someone is deciding which solutions will add the most value to the business because every recommended purchase is not practical.

Ultimately, they build a case to justify the spend. We call that value.

Is what they expect to gain from doing business with you more than they expect to spend?

Often that metric is ROI. How do you calculate ROI? You quantify the financial impact resulting from your purchase and compare it to the expense. If I expect to gain $100 cost savings as a result of a $25 purchase, my ROI is 4x or 400%. Some prospects also expect that ROI to be achieved in a specific time frame. In other words, time to value is often a consideration as well.

The key for most sales reps to understand is that value can be quantified. It can be absolute rather than relative. The value must be specific and believable. And it can be expanded in the customer's mind.

Absolute value means that I understand exactly what the quantified gain is. Relative value is a directional increase in the value proposition. It is the difference between *I will save $100* versus *there is cost savings*. Absolute value is actionable; relative value is vague.

One area that many sales reps fail to understand is all the metrics that could lead to positive value and ROI. Maybe it is cost savings. And it could also be efficiency or improved processes. Again, the savvy value seller expands the metrics that value can be attributed to by expanding the conversation to include multiple metrics, not just the obvious one.

For example, maybe you sell a SaaS solution that handles inbound leads and scheduling. You're selling to a prospect that handles inbound leads in a unique way and is dealing with limited

CRM functionality, making lead assignment difficult. After creating a custom solution, you present the 6-month roadmap for value realization.

As part of your presentation, you include the anticipated cost savings. The obvious is speed to accurate lead scoring and assignment. You share the value proposition that the ROI is 700%, and unfortunately, the buying team discounts everything you share because they don't believe the numbers and aren't convinced that they can come close to achieving this.

The moral of the story is this: ROI is a function of what the customer thinks and measures as the gain, and that gain can be any number of metrics. The sales rep's job is to understand all those metrics and quantify the impact in a conversation that involves the prospect. When an ROI calculator is used without the prospect, they will likely disbelieve the results.

And let's not forget that people have their own motivations as well. You need to connect to personal value. Individuals will not be motivated to take action on a solution that does not align with their personal, professional, and individual goals and objectives. To buy is human, and humans are motivated for their own reasons.

At the end of the day, there must be enough value to motivate change. That means all the factors that go into implementation, time/money spent, departmental priorities, organizational culture, and competing initiatives must be *worth it*.

Every organization has problems and pain—most of the time, they're perfectly happy living with this pain because the solution to alleviate it is simply not worth it. The sales professionals who create customers for life are adept at tying their product/solution to key business drivers and setting the ROI on unshakable grounds.

You should have the answers to the following questions:

- Has the prospect identified how they will measure success?
- Have they defined the expected outcomes and time frame?

- What metrics will be impacted, and what is the baseline to determine improvement?
- Does the prospect think those results are achievable?
- Is the quantified, agreed-upon value or outcome more than the investment?
- How does your business outcome impact the individual?
- Is there enough personal value to support the change?
- Does the prospect agree to the quantifiable impact?

Who Can Buy?

Have you ever heard this from someone you are selling to: *Perfect. Looks like we're in alignment on this. At this point, I'll have to run it by my boss for approval, I'll be back to you in a few days.*

Make no mistake: It doesn't matter what you're selling, if you're not talking to the ultimate decision-maker you're at risk of wasting your time.

You can't sell to someone who can't buy.

Don't get me wrong: I'm not saying to only engage the final decision-maker. Yes, engage the entire buying group, and identify who will make the decisions and how they will make it. Way back in Chapter 1, I talked about an article that came out in *Harvard Business Review* in the fall of 2022. Based on a survey of more than 1,200 B2B buyers conducted by Bain and Google,[2] they found that salespeople tend to focus on high-level decision-makers to the point where they misunderstand the makeup and influence of the entire buying committee—which is obviously a huge mistake. These individuals can provide you with valuable information and introduce you to other influential contacts within the client organization. Plus, you'll ultimately need to win them over. To close complex deals, you'll need to address each of their unique challenges, speak their language, and provide value.

I've seen this scenario play out countless times—one of the most striking examples happened in the fall of 2022. One of our top performers was working an opportunity in the fintech space. He'd managed to develop a strong rapport with the CRO who was in his first 90 days at the company. Yet, he was up against a competitor who was friends with the CEO.

Now, the CEO wanted the decision to be a joint one, seeking input from the CRO and head of enablement—and yet the competitor did not take this to heart. Relying exclusively on his relationship with the CEO, he neglected to engage the other members of the buying committee and add value. We're talking to the point where his presentation to the CRO was full of "insert client name here" prompts and had no information on how his company compared to ours—information the CRO had specifically asked to see. Needless to say, the CRO had a hard time viewing this individual as credible. In the end, he threw down a mandate to the CEO: "If you hire him, I walk." It goes to show how vital it is to always add value in every interaction with every stakeholder who can influence the deal.

When it comes to internal champions, I get it. It's incredibly tempting to cling to these individuals and follow their lead. After all, you don't want to compromise your rapport with them by going over their head. Plus, they know the internal politics of their company far better than you—maybe you should trust that they have everything in hand. Moreover, forging a new relationship with an executive-level decision-maker is fraught with potential pitfalls, and even if it does go smoothly, the time investment is significant.

Hard stop. If you're not at power, the deal is at risk. Power might have a preference for another vendor or a different perspective on what the problems are—you'll never know without access. As we'll discuss in Chapter 11, there are tactics you can use to access power and accelerate your relationship with these individuals. However, it's key to put a plan into action for engaging these individuals sooner rather than later, and if that proves improbable, it might be time to move on.

You should have the answers to the following questions:

- Does this purchase price logically fit with the prospect's authority level?
- Do you understand their decision-making process?
- Who is involved in the decision?
- Who is the final decision-maker?
- Once the decision is made, who executes the decision?

When Will They Buy?

We've already won! I'm only waiting on the CXO to sign, and she's on vacation for two weeks.

It's with legal, and they have a deadline for reviewing contracts that no one knew about.

We got the verbal, but procurement has taken over the decision.

What do all of these have in common? They're all examples of what you might hear when you lack insight into the prospect's buying process. And it's vital that you understand every step along the way if you want to avoid costly surprises. To build your knowledge and mitigate risk, work with the buyer to outline a two-way understanding of a company's crucial business issues and the activities required to resolve them—and put it in writing. This mutual plan is a powerful tool for building confidence in buying decisions.

A critical component of the plan is a timeline that the buyer agrees to—and one that includes milestones and specificity on what has to happen before, during, and after the purchase. The timeline begins with the end in mind. The end from the prospect's point of view is the outcomes they expect from your product or service. This plan backs into all of the steps, milestones, and activities that must happen in order to get there.

And in the next chapter, I'll detail a painless way to quickly craft them and incorporate the process into your daily workflows.

You should have the answers to the following questions:

- Does the timeline map to the time-bound business issue?
- Does the timeline include the timing of expected outcomes or value?
- Does the timeline end with the positive outcome expected by the prospect?
- Does the timeline include all of the necessary departmental reviews, e.g., legal, procurement, and data compliance?
- Are these departments aware of the timeline?
- Is the timeline agreed to in writing?

■ ■ ■

When you combine all of the listed elements, you're left with one powerful framework for prospect qualification—we call it the Qualified Prospect Formula® (QP Formula) and it breaks down as shown in Figure 9.3.

Notice that equation is based on multiplication—that's because if one of the elements mentioned earlier equals zero, the

The Qualified Prospect Formula

$$QP = VM_D \times V \times P \times P^{®}$$

Qualified Prospect =

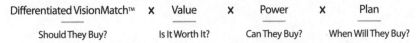

Differentiated VisionMatch™	×	Value	×	Power	×	Plan
Should They Buy?		Is It Worth It?		Can They Buy?		When Will They Buy?

Figure 9.3 The Qualified Prospect Formula.

Source: ValueSelling Associates, https://www.slideshare.net/ValueSellingAssociates/valueselling-associates-august-2019-webinar-on-prospecting-and-qualifying/ (last accessed April 24, 2023).

whole equation equals zero, and the opportunity is unqualified. A zero qualified prospect is an indication that key information is unconfirmed or unknown and places this opportunity at risk. Use this process to evaluate all of your opportunities to build a sustainable revenue pipeline you can count on. As counterintuitive as it may sound, this checklist is the most crucial at the times when you're the most convinced the opportunity will close. When you're sure the deal will close is when you must be the most vigilant.

In the end, we can only eliminate risk from the forecast when we qualify the prospect through this lens, and it's all based upon the timeline that the prospect has shared with us. When you focus on qualified prospects with a defined timeline, forecast accuracy improves—and a qualified prospect must have a timeline that maps to the forecast period.

How often do you need to qualify and requalify? Every time something changes. And the longer the sales cycle, the more things will change. This is a continuous process, not a one-time checklist or event.

IV

Enable the Buying Process

10

Reverse Engineering the Buying Process

Throughout my career, I've seen countless definitions of the sales profession. There's one that resonates with me the most: *Sales is the facilitation of buying via the transference of confidence from the seller to the buyer.*

And according to Todd Caponi, it's not that the buyer has confidence because you have convinced them—the buyer has confidence because they can predict the experience or outcomes of doing business with you.

The key to this definition is that the core of any successful sales engagement focuses on the buyer's success at completing a purchase. In most B2B buying processes, the buying company typically goes through six phases:

1. Identifying problems
2. Searching for information and options
3. Evaluating alternatives
4. Justifying the expenditure
5. Purchasing
6. Evaluating the solution post-purchase

Notice that nowhere in this process is a sales professional explicitly included.

That's the dilemma for most sales reps today—how do you synchronize the buying process to your selling process? The first step, of course, is to ensure you understand the buying process.

Gartner has shared two troubling and conflicting statistics that only complicate this challenge:

1. Fifty-six percent of buyers[1] have significant purchase regret after a large technology purchase.
2. Buyers, on average, spend 17% of their time with potential suppliers—that means they only spend 5% to 6% of their time meeting with an individual seller.[2]

It's intriguing that buyers who don't rely on vendor or supplier salespeople during their decision process are often unhappy with the decision they make. That's a potentially disastrous situation from a customer retention and brand image perspective—one that all revenue teams should be working to eliminate. To increase your odds of success and create reasons for your customers to stay, you'll need to closely align with *their* processes and preferences. That begins by meeting buyers wherever they are in their journey.

Meet Buyers Where They Are

If you expect to add value to the buying journey, you first need to understand where the buyer is in that journey.

Who is the buyer?

What is the role of this project or initiative?

What stage are they currently in?

Without this knowledge, you will be incredibly challenged to add value. After all, the most significant opportunity you have is to resynchronize your selling process to the prospect's buying process. To do that, you'll need a developed under-standing of the buyers and their unique journey.

■ ■ ■

Often a vendor or supplier is invited into a buying process roughly halfway through the process—the customer had identified problems, challenges, or an opportunity to change. This opportunity could be a number of different things. They could be firing a current supplier and shopping for alternatives, or they might have recognized that a current process is no longer serving their needs. Finally, they could be exploring a completely new paradigm or solution that had never existed before.

Each of these scenarios demands a different response from the sales professional.

When you are displacing an incumbent supplier, contrast is critical. Identifying the differences between you and competitive alternatives is a key component of what your buyer wants and requires. In these situations, you're typically invited to the conversation later in the buying journey—the buyer has likely made the decision to change and sought out options and alternatives. Education is the focus here, and the buyers may believe they are already educated as they have purchased similar products and services before. As we've already covered, they may be or they may not be—you'll need to test the waters to know how the buyers came to the conclusion that they did.

To do this, you must reverse engineer the "why"—the moving forces that triggered the exploration of solutions in the first place: *What problems do they expect to solve? What about the incumbent solution—what do they like, and what is causing frustration?*

In these instances, buyers may have developed a very complete list of requirements or identified needs. Have you ever been a recipient of an RFP or spreadsheet with a laundry list of capabilities?

There's a big problem with this: Buyers aren't always adept at self-diagnosis. The same could be said of physicians—most are notoriously horrible at diagnosing their own diseases. Why is this? It's because they're too close to the situation to see the forest through the trees—the same is true of our buyers and prospects. In contrast, buyers often believe they have a complete picture of what is needed. Maybe it is complete. More often than not, it is incomplete.

The gap you'll struggle with is understanding *why* those capabilities are needed. You must identify the reason why those capabilities are required. When the solution conversation is preceded by a thorough conversation on the problems, the solution will be more relevant in the buyer's mind.

Every problem can be solved in a few different ways. For example, if I don't have the in-house expertise to do something, I have alternatives available to me. I can hire the experience; I can train my team; or I can outsource the work to a third party. As a sales professional, I don't only want to know what the buyer thinks the solution is, I also want to fully understand *why* they need it.

The classic dilemma for sales professionals is how to back up prospects in their thought process while identifying opportunities to re-educate and the context needed to position your solution as the best alternative.

Most organizations I work with do a very good job of ensuring their sales reps are proficient in the functionality/features of the products and services they sell. If the product is complex, they develop expertise to support the sales rep: sales engineers, product specialists, and other SMEs become part of the sales team. This expertise is very inwardly focused, tied to technical explanations of the nuances and uniqueness of your products and built upon use cases that bring your service to life in a way that the buyer understands.

However, this inward focus of the sales team is not complete or adequate.

Buyers become frustrated when sales professionals don't understand their business, their needs, and their desired outcomes. Sales reps show up ready to demo and explain and fail to make connections to the buyer. They show up and throw up and run the risk of talking about functionality that the buyer doesn't care about. Don't fall into this trap.

Your Solution *Is* Important

It goes without saying that effective sales professionals know their own products and services inside and out—that's the price of admission to sales success.

However, your solution must solve a problem worth solving for a prospect. The key to resynchronizing the buying process is to understand the problems that their shopping list of capabilities is meant to address. As you prepare for the sales conversation, work to understand the buyer journey before you were involved. In the conversations themselves, you need to back the buyer up and ask them to open up about the process—while being cautious to not annoy them.

As we discussed in previous chapters, targeted questioning techniques and the ability to ask thought-provoking questions unlock fruitful business conversations. When attempting to begin a dialogue around the elements of the buying process that took place before you were involved, start with these questions:

- *What led you to reach out to us today?*
- *Will you please share the process/journey you have been on to this point?*

The key is to let the buyer do the talking to get the information you need.

For example, I once was working with a client in the logistics industry. They were struggling to differentiate their solution from the competition. The sales professionals approached each opportunity with five to eight key points they wanted to tell their prospects about their proposed solution. They asked no questions—they assumed there was a need for their solutions and wanted to pitch or present as quickly as possible.

As a result, they were failing. Buyers thought they were arrogant. They talked and talked and didn't listen. Potential buyers hated the experience, and the sales reps were losing market share.

One of the sales reps asked me, *Why should I ask questions? I already know what the answers are.* She missed the point. It doesn't matter if you know the answer. What matters is that the prospect connects the capabilities you have to the challenges they acknowledge. Eliminating assumptions is key to making direct connections and establishing your solution as the best option.

To reinvent their approach, they frontloaded the conversation with questions to gain insight into the buyer and their situation. Now that the focus wasn't on their capabilities but on the buyer's perspective, prospects leaned into the conversations; sales reps became more proficient at tailoring their solution discussions to the salient points that the individual prospect cared about; they stopped overwhelming the prospect with information they didn't need to make a good decision.

■ ■ ■

Becoming a problem expert is more important than becoming a solution expert.

Let me give you an example of what I mean. I read a story on LinkedIn written by a consultant who shared a valuable lesson he'd just learned by losing a sale.

In a sales call, the prospect shared a problem that he wanted to solve. The consultant was thrilled because his solution was an immediate match, and he immediately went on to share how he could address the problem. He flipped the switch and dove into demo mode, describing his tools and platform, walked through a use case, and was convinced that he would win the sale based on the strength of his capabilities.

A week later, the consultant received an email thanking him for his time and letting him know that he was not a fit.

Why did the consultant lose this sale?

He didn't diagnose before he prescribed—he pitched a blood pressure pill to treat chronic headaches. Don't get me wrong: He had a great solution and should be proud of what he had developed. Still, he failed to identify *all* of the reasons that his prospect was shopping and dove into capabilities.

The most shocking part of the story?

He knew better. He readily admitted he should have extended discovery—yet the allure of jumping into "fix it" mode was simply too great. And this is the primary struggle salespeople face. We are understandably excited about the products/services we sell; we know them inside and out; we've seen the results we bring to clients. Plus, it's tempting to fall back on product knowledge because it's comfortable. Every sales call is full of unknown variables—product knowledge is certain, and we're comfortable talking about it. And that's your biggest potential pitfall.

Say it with me: *Selling isn't telling—it's connecting*. And to connect, we need to understand the buyers and meet them where they are. Every solution must solve a problem. When we work with clients, we spend a lot of classroom time on this reverse engineering process. We know the sales reps are well versed and trained in their solutions, and because of that, we start there.

We ask sellers to make a list of the unique capabilities. We then expand that list to incorporate the various buyers and their competitors in an attempt to examine which capabilities will matter more or less to the distinct personas. Then we ask, "So what?" We ask the sales reps to figure out what a client would have to need, or what problem they would want to solve, for that capability to matter to them.

For instance, one thing that ValueSelling Associates offers is localized and translated training in multiple languages. For some clients, that is a necessity. For others, it is irrelevant. Our "so what" for that capability is understanding if a client has a global sales team that requires local language training. We teach our sales reps to probe for that circumstance or challenge. If it exists, great! We'll include information about our global reach. If it doesn't exist, we don't discuss it.

This process is critical to understanding the problems/ circumstances you're trying to uncover to correctly position your solution. To prepare for our sales conversations, we start with the solution because we know the most about that. We then go back into the problems we can solve.

To execute sales conversations, we flip this around. We first probe for the problems, and when we have a complete understanding, we move to the solution. Ultimately, the more problems we can uncover, the higher the likelihood of three things:

1. We can better differentiate among the alternatives.
2. We deepen our understanding and build trust by focusing on the prospect's agenda, not merely our own agenda.
3. We enable ourselves to craft a larger solution to solve multiple problems.

Differentiation

Being differentiated is not the same as being different or unique.

Differentiation is the process of making your product or service better than similar options in your prospects' unique situation. The interesting thing about differentiation is that it is a buyer-specific determination. Every buyer may deem different components of your solution valuable. Differentiation is therefore not a universal statement; it is a conclusion we work to ensure the prospect comes to on their own.

Here's an example: I have a client who sells payroll services. And you might think that processing payroll is a straightforward solution. Some view it as a commodity and seek to select the least expensive alternative. However, if something has ever gone wrong with your payroll, you understand that it is not merely a tool for paying people accurately—it's tied into compliance, taxes, reporting, and other factors that can cause serious headaches for businesses.

Our client quickly came to the realization that when their prospects were only buying payroll, it was nearly impossible to differentiate. All of the payroll providers provided very similar services. They also discovered that there were two areas where they could excel.

First, they had a tremendous customer service model. Unlike their competitors, they had dedicated customer service representatives assigned to each client. These customer service reps not only responded to issues, they proactively developed relationships to anticipate client needs and address them before they became a problem. Clients were provided a name and a direct phone number should they need service. Their competitors had customer service too—an 800 number and an integrated voice response system.

You can see the difference straight away. We taught the sales reps how to probe for problems related to customer service—they'd ask questions like the following:

- *Have you ever found it difficult to reach a live person when you had a problem?*
- *Is it challenging not having direct access to a rep who can help you?*
- *Do you get frustrated when you have to repeat information multiple times to get to someone who can solve the issue?*

Two interesting things happened: First, when the payroll salespeople began asking these questions, they found out if their customer service model would be relevant to the prospect.

If they had positive responses to these probing questions, they could educate the prospect on their unique approach, contrasting their offering to the alternatives. The second intriguing development was that sellers began to understand that there can be multiple questions to identify a problem or circumstance for their solution. In the earlier examples, those three questions are all tied to one solution element. The questions are all trying to uncover something similar, and any one of these could open up a need for the customer service model.

In addition, they also realized they had capabilities way beyond payroll—they could provide human resources (HR) support, benefit options, worker's compensation, and many other capabilities. Yet, the salespeople thought of those options as afterthoughts and add-ons as opposed to the core offering that could drive differentiation.

By changing the mindset of the sellers from selling payroll to selling comprehensive compensation and HR solutions, we fundamentally changed the way they approached potential clients. We turned the salespeople into problem experts. They didn't stop discovery when a single issue was uncovered regarding payroll. Instead, they invested the time to uncover additional opportunities for the full breadth of their solution to be relevant. After developing a list of all the areas they would investigate with all new prospects, they deliberately included those questions in every ongoing discovery process. It sounds simple—and the results were profound.

They began winning more and winning bigger opportunities. Before they worked with us, 20% of their deals included HR services and benefits. After the mindset and process change, 60% of the opportunities included two or more product lines.

Notice that their capabilities didn't change—the differences that had always existed became relevant because of the approach of their sales professionals.

It goes to show you that when most of us think of being different, we think about our product. *Do we have something to offer that is unique in the marketplace?* Don't get me wrong—when that happens, it's awesome. It's also extremely challenging to sustain. Knockoffs show up time and time again, and our competitors continue advancing their capabilities.

Differentiation must go beyond product capabilities. To begin your search for the differences that matter to your buyer, examine three areas:

1. **Customer Experience:** Today's buyer expects the buying process and the vendor relationship to be easy. We have all been conditioned by e-commerce giants to expect immediacy and accessibility. CX is the totality of what a customer encounters as they engage with you. Your overall experience with your prospects must add meaningful value. Today, that experience must be frictionless—it must be intuitive and easy to navigate.

2. **Terms and Conditions:** When there is parity between competitive products/solutions, clients may differentiate on the basis of terms and conditions. Terms and conditions are the legal agreements between companies when they agree to work with each other. They cover everything from when and how you pay, warranties, ownership of work product, privacy and security, and numerous other elements.

   I've seen clients differentiate on warranties and guarantees and on frequency and payment terms. For example, a vendor who is willing to invoice quarterly may be a better fit than a vendor who expects an upfront payment. For some clients and opportunities, these terms could be *the differentiator*.

   Shared risk investment models are another example. Under certain circumstances, my company will tie a portion of our compensation and total fees to the results a client realizes because of our partnership. This term reduces the upfront fees a client will pay us, and we agree to a sliding scale on the remaining balance based on the agreed-upon measurable outcomes the client achieves.

3. **Risk Mitigation:** A key differentiator for certain companies and brands is risk mitigation. This is the perception—by the buyer—that the alternative is the least risky option. They might base this perception on a vendor's track record for success, its market position, the thought leadership of the executive team, or the references of well-known companies that also use your products/services.

Risk mitigation today is a key component of the buyer journey. When doing online research, the buyer seeks product and company reviews—they ask for information and experiences from social networks and online peer groups.

Companies that differentiate in this vector have an established mechanism for cultivating online reviews, customer stories, and relevant testimonials. Many vendors also work to build credibility through associations with well-known companies that have chosen to work with them.

Ultimately, when differentiation is not clear, the deal breaker is price. That is the definition of a pure commodity.

The savvy buyer today will work to minimize your differentiation in order to negotiate the best price. After all, it's the buyer's job.

The process of differentiation and the discovery of what is important to the buyer has to happen prior to any negotiation. Once your price and terms are on the table, it is too late to back up and expand discovery.

■   ■   ■

Your prospects crave to be seen and heard. They need you to understand why they are different and why they are seeking unique solutions. They set the criteria—our opportunity is to expand that list of criteria with thought-provoking questions. Becoming a problem expert and deliberately reverse engineering the buying process is the key to your ability to successfully run any sales process.

11

Speak Value to Power

You don't have to be an executive's peer to sell to the C-suite.

Over the course of my career, I've seen sales professionals fall prey to that thinking again and again—it's by far the biggest roadblock. They tend to be intimidated by the differences: They focus on differences in age, pay grade, experience, business expertise, and countless other factors. They assume the executive has better things to do with their time than meeting with sales professionals. As a result, they fear the interaction, and this manifests as avoidance.

The magic happens when you flip your mindset and start investigating the similarities. Yes, every company and executive is unique—and the mechanisms and motivations that facilitate their buying processes are eerily similar.

The secret to selling to the C-suite is being relevant, credible, and engaging executives in business conversations. As we talked about in Chapter 5, this all starts with speaking the language of executives. To engage at this level, your expertise must go beyond product knowledge—you'll need a working understanding of business and financial terms to understand how a business operates and get a glimpse into its current state. After all, from an executive's perspective, the value of these conversations isn't merely the outcomes offered by your product/solution, but the conversation itself. C-level executives seek business advisors who can share novel insights and actionable ideas to expand their thinking.

For the purposes of this chapter, I'm assuming you've already read Chapter 5 or have a developed understanding of how businesses operate and the business acumen to investigate their financials. If not, I encourage you to go back and read through it—it's an excellent primer for this discussion. In Chapter 5, I covered the strategy for thinking like an executive. Here, I'll build upon that foundation and walk through the tactical aspects of identifying power, gaining access, selling on value, and closing the deal.

Why Sell to the C-suite?

I hear you: *What's in it for me? Why should I invest the time and energy into selling to C-suite executives to begin with?* Because you stand to gain five game-changing advantages:

1. **A Solid Understanding of Business Drivers and Issues:** Your whole objective is to understand the business issues that are getting in the way of the company's goals and map the value of your product/solution to them. Want a better understanding of the high-level business strategy and the challenges to implementing it? Talk to the person who set that strategy to begin with. Sure, any director or vice president will be happy to tell you all about what the C-suite wants to accomplish—and you'll hear as many versions as there are people. Do you remember the telephone example from Chapter 9 on forecasting? Well, imagine that playing out across a large corporation, comprised of individuals who all have unique personal and professional motivations. Yikes! Far better to start at the source.

2. **A Credible Reputation:** By now, you're convinced that credibility, trust, and rapport are essential to closing sales—and an introduction from the C-suite can go a long way to helping you build all three with individuals across the organization. Most B2B buyers are inundated with outreach, and most of it is lost to the void of spam or gets deleted. However, when a message comes down from the C-suite to other buyers in the organization that it's worth their time to speak with you, it strikes a whole different note.

3. **Access to the Whole Organization:** A C-suite executive must take a broad view of the business—use this to your advantage by formulating a need for your product/solution on the organizational level from the very beginning instead of selling into a specific department. The result is typically a substantially larger deal size. Plus, by taking this organizational view, you're in a better position to see all of the moving pieces, identify every need, and maximize client value—the foundation for creating customers for life.

4. **Quicker Qualification and Sales Cycles:** If a C-level executive is on board, that's a crucial element to check off the Qualified Prospect Formula and often hints that the other elements are soon to follow. Or they might not be interested at all, but at least you know you're working an unqualified opportunity sooner rather than after months of work. Sales cycles also tend to be shorter since you're dealing with an individual who's responsible for driving the business forward and paid to make decisions quickly—they need impacts, and they need them yesterday.

    In addition, if you can get into the sales process early enough, you can help shape the criteria for the final decision—stacking the comparisons in a way that eliminates your competition.

5. **Easier Sales Calls:** Executive buyers crave high-level business conversations—they want to talk about eliminating problems and maximizing value. In contrast, when you're

dealing with a technical buyer or SME, they will dissect the solution and challenge even the minutest aspects of your solution.

Why Is Identifying the Ultimate Decision-maker so Difficult?

You're determined to engage the final decision-maker in a productive business conversation that piques their interest, establishes trust, expands their thinking, and identifies critical business challenges that your solution can solve. Great . . . only, who should you actually call?

It's a phenomenal question. One that's only compounded by the fact that many salespeople fool themselves into believing that someone other than the final decision-maker can sufficiently sell for them internally. Sure, sometimes it works out—more commonly, it does not. In addition, it's all too commonplace for a prospect to say they have purchasing power, work with you throughout the sales process, and come to an agreement on problems worth solving and the value your solution will provide— only to admit at the last minute that they don't have the authority to sign the purchase order. Or they may genuinely not understand how purchases of this magnitude are made at their company. Whatever the reason, if you find yourself at this junction, you're not merely back at the starting line, you're lying in bed the night before thinking about the race. You've lost critical time, wasted valuable energy, and burned through the majority of your patience in the process.

You also have to consider how businesses operate in times of uncertainty. When companies become risk-averse, the first order of business is adding more checks and balances to the purchasing process. In my experience, since 2020, the number of people involved from higher levels in the organization has skyrocketed. You're probably looking at a minimum of four people involved in small decisions, with that number going into the 20s or 30s for complex deals at large, global organizations. When you're dealing with such an extensive buying group, you need to be clear on who has power, exactly how much they have, and what kind it is.

Keep in mind that power isn't always denoted by the senior title. Who holds power will vary drastically depending on the company's size and structure. A senior vice president at a company with 52 employees probably carries less decision-making authority than a director at an Adobe or Intuit who oversees a few hundred individuals. Don't just look at a person's title on LinkedIn—closely examine their roles, responsibilities, and span of control.

Another aspect of power to consider is who has the political power to get things done. Internal politics often determine who the ultimate decision-maker is. For example, a vice president of sales and a vice president of marketing might be fighting for funds from the same budget. Cover your bets and do the work to craft a VisionMatch with both of them, tying it to their respective personal values.

In addition to the previous scenarios, you'll also need to watch out for three common stumbling blocks:

- Misunderstanding power structures: Unlike the previous example, this individual genuinely believes he has the power to buy, but he actually doesn't.
- Assuming interest is power: Don't fall into the trap of thinking, *If she takes the meeting, she must be the decision-maker*.
- Conflating budgets with final decision-making authority: Depending on the company, the individual with the budget to fund an initiative may not be the final decision-maker. For example, a vice president of sales might have the budget to fund sales training *and* need approval from the CEO to actually buy.

Rest assured: Whatever you're dealing with, there's a way around it—and it's worth it. Ultimately, the heart of value selling is mitigating risk and maximizing selling time. It's essential to gain access to and confirm you are dealing with the individual who has the authority to act. In the corporate world, there are many people who can say, "No." Only accept a "no" if it comes from the person who could have said, "Yes."

Who Actually Has Power?

Don't be the sales rep from Chapter 9: Never, never discount the influence of everyone involved in the buying decision. Your goal to establish a business relationship with the final decision-maker shouldn't affect your ability to engage the entire buying committee—in fact, it should only facilitate it.

Asking the same questions to multiple people inside the organization is a potent and simple way to ensure your perspective is accurate. This process is based on a concept called triangulation; you compare and contrast multiple sources of information to verify the truth. Use it in your search for the ultimate decision-maker by questioning the contacts you make at various levels. Sure, their responses will probably vary, and that doesn't mean that people are being untruthful, but that people have different perspectives depending on their area of expertise and where they sit in the organization. Still, by comparing three or four answers, you should be able to determine who holds purchasing authority. Remember: Do so carefully and respectfully and never compromise your rapport with any of these individuals—they may not have the authority to say, "Yes," but they can always say, "No."

Use the following questions to identify power:

- Who else besides you is involved in the decision?
- Who else is affected by this decision?
- Who has the budget to fund this initiative?
- What or who could stop this initiative?

- How have decisions and purchases of this magnitude been made in the past?
- Have you sought approval for a purchase on this scale in the past?
- Once the final decision is made, what happens next?
- Is there anyone who could veto your decision?
- If you had to get more funding, who would you turn to?

The process of triangulation not only helps you identify power—it also helps you avoid a potentially disastrous habit that all salespeople should break: relying on a single-buyer contact. Ask yourself: *What happens if your only contact is let go, transferred, or resigns?* I'll tell you what happens, you're dead in the water—but at least, you're in good company. According to LinkedIn's State of Sales 2022 report,[1] 86% of sellers lost a deal or had it delayed in the preceding year by a decision-maker changing roles. To avoid this trap, you need to identify all stakeholders who will influence the deal and multithread the engagement by establishing a unique business relationship with all of them.

These stakeholders generally fit into four buckets: economic thinkers, influencers, sponsors/coaches, and end users. Your economic thinkers are concerned with . . . you guessed it, the economic impact. These individuals are responsible for getting the most from the organization's investment, and while they may handle the negotiating and actual procurement, they won't actually use the product. You'll also find that they aren't too interested in hearing about your solution's true value to the overall organization—their goal is to limit differentiation to price alone.

Influencers represent the other members of the buying group who might use the product themselves and/or gather input from the end users. They too have the clout to say, "No," but not the authority to say, "Yes."

A sponsor/coach is someone who has been tasked with doing the evaluation or groundwork and is ultimately going to make a recommendation to the power person. They can provide you with perspective and feedback on the internal processes you're not privy to—they have both access and knowledge and may or may not be a part of the buying group. They are the ones sharing insights to help you win.

Cultivating this relationship effectively can lead to a great payout. For instance, I've had coaches in deals who go as far as texting me the chief sales officer's questions in meetings, so I can provide a tailored response in real time.

Finally, you'll encounter the end user. These buyers are often SMEs and inclined to examine the functionality of your product/solution from all angles. Ensure you understand the functionality or approach requirements they have in mind and demonstrate how your solution maps to them.

In addition to the earlier examples, every deal may contain a saboteur—these individuals are aligned to another solution and actively work to undermine your case from within. If this happens, work with your coach to further understand this person's role, fears, and motivations to find ways to neutralize them. For instance, my sellers often encounter internal trainers who are threatened by the prospect of an outside methodology company. Educating these individuals on the opportunities we provide to certify in-house trainers works to neutralize their antagonism and assure them that we are not a threat to their place in the organization.

You'll interact with all of these buying group "types" over the course of the buying process. To effectively earn the buy-in of every member of the team, ensure you educate and engage all stakeholders in the manner that's appropriate to them. By working with each individual to understand their view of business issues, problems, solutions, and value, you will be able to develop a VisionMatch that connects with their individual perspectives and turns them into advocates for your solution.

As you engage and educate the buying committee, always remember one thing: The power person is the ultimate decision-maker—they have the final decision and the most to win or lose with your solution, so you must find a way to connect with them. Before you can do that, you'll need access, so let's look at how you'll leverage referrals, bypass gatekeepers, bargain and campaign for access, and ultimately maintain that hard-won access to close more deals, faster.

Quick win: Even as you work strategically with influencers and sponsors, remember that your success or failure ultimately hinges on your relationship with power. Do not expect anyone else to sell on your behalf.

Gaining Access to Power

Before I detail the tactics you'll use to gain executive access, we have to talk about the giant, pink elephant in the room: self-sabotage.

Some sales reps avoid calling higher altogether—either from intimidation, lack of confidence, or fear of ridicule—because they're concerned they will not be able to add value and will lose the deal outright. Whatever the reason may be, this puts them at a tremendous disadvantage. And their concerns are often misplaced. After all, as long as you've done your research and can efficiently evaluate the company's financials to identify trends (if not, see Chapter 5!), you have nothing to lose. The higher up you go, the easier it is to have a business conversation because, at that level, it's all about the bottom line and less about the nitty-gritty technical specs and details of your product/solution. With that said, you'll probably only get one shot, which is why it's imperative you come prepared.

With that out of the way, let's dive into the mechanics of accessing the C-suite.

Referrals

When it comes to executive access, the most dependable tool at your disposal is referrals. Think: *Who do you know? Who knows them? Who do they respect?* Ideally, this will end in an introduction, and it might take other useful forms. For instance, maybe the person in your network isn't comfortable brokering an introduction, but they have valuable intel to share on the prospect and their reputation. Or perhaps, they'd be willing to offer you an endorsement on LinkedIn to bolster your credibility.

As I said, the ideal outcome is an email or LinkedIn message introducing you to the target executive. Personally, I must delete at least 50 cold outreach emails daily, but if someone from my network says, *Hey Julie, I know someone it would be worth taking 15 minutes to speak to,* I will always take the meeting. If you're fortunate enough to get to this point, follow up with urgency and respect. Your network contact went out on a limb to introduce you to this senior executive; if you don't follow up with urgency, it might damage their credibility in the eyes of this executive. Also, don't forget to thank your connection as soon as possible— sending a small gift is a nice touch and ensures they know their contribution is valued.

Maybe you're early in your career and don't have a well-developed network of contacts connected to the C-suite—that's perfectly fine because you can always leverage relationships with current and former customers. In fact, the 2022 study done by Bain and Google[2] that I mentioned in Chapter 9 highlighted a known, and often overlooked, phenomenon: Buyers depend on recommendations from their peers. With this in mind, normalize the process of asking your clients for referrals today. Worst case, they say, "No." Best case, they say, "Yes, I know two people you should reach out to immediately."

Quick win: Use software like the LinkedIn SalesNavigator TeamLink feature to see if any employees at your company are connected to the prospect and would be willing to introduce you.

Bypassing Gatekeepers

Without a direct introduction, you'll likely run into a gatekeeper at one stage or another in the buying process. While these individuals don't have buying power, they certainly have veto power, or at the very least, they can attempt to place an immovable wall between you and your goal. Always, always treat these individuals with respect and recognize they hold the keys. Instead of treating them as obstacles, treat them as allies.

You will likely run up against two distinct types of human gatekeepers: administrative assistants and middle managers. When you're dealing with administrative assistants, the first step is to understand that they're merely doing their jobs—they're supposed to screen calls and meetings to guard an executive's time, and they're very good at it. Because of their role, they'll have tremendous insight into the target executive's mindset, plans, and priorities—these individuals can quickly become your best friends if you play your cards right. In contrast, if you're rude or rush the interaction, you can count on the executive learning about your behavior and never taking your call. When engaging these admins, your best bet is to be direct and ask for help. For instance, if I was calling on an executive at a manufacturing company and reached an administrative assistant, I might say:

> *Hi, this is Julie Thomas from ValueSelling Associates.*
>
> *My company works with manufacturing companies like [COMPANY NAME] to drive sales productivity and effectiveness. Under what circumstances would your chief sales officer be willing to take a meeting?*

Sometimes, that's all it takes.

Back in 2020, one of my associates was selling into a data analytics company and attempted to connect with its senior vice president of sales. He had leveraged the Vortex Prospecting program and already sent two emails using the A-I-M framework that contained intriguing third-party insights. Going into the second week of outreach, he switched to the phone and the senior vice president's administrative assistant answered. He explained the purpose of his call, being careful to reference the information he'd sent over and what his goals were. The admin listened and instead of transferring him to the senior vice president, he put the associate through to the head of enablement. Why? Well, he'd been in a meeting with the senior vice president of sales and head of enablement that very morning—he'd seen everything play out and knew that sales effectiveness was top-of-mind for the head of enablement and that he was charged with implementing a solution. My associate was able to add value to the enablement lead in their initial conversation, and the opportunity closed less than 2 months later—easily saving the associate a tremendous amount of time that he would have spent attempting to establish a relationship with the senior vice president when the head of enablement had the power from the very beginning.

Quick win: *Avoid voicemail. Human-to-human connection is the way to go. Ask if the person you want to talk with is actually in the office, what's the best time for reaching them, and what's the best way to set an appointment.*

The next gatekeeper you'll encounter is a middle manager who's been authorized to explore alternatives or evaluate options but lacks final decision-making power. In my experience, these individuals come in two guises: On the one hand, you have the middle manager who craves information because it conveys a certain power to them. On the other, you have middle managers who are doing their own thing and not as plugged into a larger initiative or need as they may seem. The first type is easy to engage and bargain with—but be wary about getting stuck with the second type because you might wind up at a dead end. The overarching approach for working with these gatekeepers is the same: *How can you partner with this individual to gain access to the ultimate decision-maker?*

As any good interviewer or teacher knows, setting expectations early can make a world of difference. During the very first meeting with a mid-level prospect, set the expectation that you need to meet with the CFO, CIO, CEO, or other top executives who are most impacted by the success of the project or involved in the decision-making process. It can be as simple as presenting it as your sales organization's modus operandi: *Our standard engagement model includes an interview with all of the project's stakeholders early on in the process.* Be careful to apply this tactic right from the start. Once you're fully engaged in the buying cycle, it's difficult to go back and say, *Oh, by the way, I forgot to mention that I need to talk to your executives before we go any further.* That's nothing but a jarring moment that's likely to erode rapport and damage your chances. And if you take this route, you have to mean it—be prepared to walk if the access you requested isn't granted.

Alternatively, you might use the power you have to bargain for access. Yes, you read that right, *your* power. While it's true that sellers no longer control the flow of information, it's debatable if a true state of information parity exists between buyers and sellers. For example, a buyer might know all there is to know about your product from a technical standpoint, but how much could they possibly know about best practices for rolling it out across their marketing, sales, and enablement functions simultaneously? Sure, they could use the same playbook they've used for other solutions. The problem with that approach is this: When you're dealing with a large complex purchase that has the power to affect the entire organization, how many times will the average B2B buyer complete such a purchase and implementation? Maybe once every 2 years, or perhaps only once or twice over the course of their career. On the sales side, you have account executives at enterprise SaaS companies who might only have 2 to 3 years of sales experience and run 12–15 of these organization-wide implementations each and every year. When you make the leap from seller to trusted business advisor, you have both valuable expertise and power—use them to your advantage to access purchasing power on the buyer's side.

Start by identifying what the mid-level prospect values that they don't have and barter with them for executive access. One of the most effective tactics is to negotiate what we call a top-to-top meeting. Offer to bring an executive from your company to the next meeting with the gatekeeper and the target executive from their company—it's a tremendous way to increase your credibility while setting the middle manager at ease. Other examples include trading things for time with the power person, bargaining chips like an extensive demonstration, a detailed ROI analysis, site visits, extended trials, or anything else that would cost your company significant time, money, or resources to provide. You might say something like this: *"If I provide a bespoke demonstration of all the facets of this system along with an ROI analysis, will you arrange a meeting for me with your CIO?"* You're probably wondering what bargaining chips you have at your disposal—start here:

- Information that's not publicly available—whether it's client-specific, an internal roadmap of panned solution upgrades, etc.
- Expertise—taking the previous example, this might be an implementation journey roadmap or consultative advice on a business process issue the prospect is facing.
- Access to satisfied customers—speaking with clients who have been in their shoes is a fantastic way to build trust and open the doors to power.
- Extended trials, customized environments, and loaner equipment/services—here again, access to solutions that solve smaller, immediate needs are a highly effective option.
- Embellished deliverables—items like the bespoke ROI analysis are tremendous tools for instilling confidence.
- Pre-sales support—bringing in an SME from your organization to answer outstanding questions and walk through technical implementation.

Keep in mind that some of these gatekeepers are trying to hold onto power as a political play, and others are attempting to mitigate risk. As with referrals, the person making the introduction to the C-suite takes on a degree of responsibility. Gatekeepers who are new to their role or unsure of their place in the organization may seek to delay involving the final decision-maker because they're nervous about taking that next step. Whatever the case, be very careful about this gatekeeper's ego—and never stop trying to gain access to the true power. At the end of the day, you always have the option of attempting to access power directly. If the previous tactics fail to produce results, consider going around this individual. It's risky. You could damage your relationship with that person beyond repair, but if you can't access purchasing power, the sale is already at risk.

Of course, when you don't have any access, the tactics mentioned earlier don't apply. Instead, dive into the Vortex Prospecting approach from Chapter 7, use the A-I-M framework and err on the side of adding value and an intriguing perspective. And be patient—remember that establishing access takes time. That first meeting alone could take 17 touches over the course of 22 business days. Always be genuine and respectful in this persistence too. However, one email with a subject line like, *Do you still want to connect on a call next Thursday?*, when the prospect has no idea what you're talking about will obliterate your credibility and chances.

Maintaining Access to Power

Alright, you've secured your golden ticket to the C-suite and established relationships with the people who have the ultimate decision-making authority . . . only to be sent back into the depths of the organization. What now?

Well, before you go traipsing off to the basement with a flashlight, negotiate a return ticket to the top. This can take the form of planned or conditional access. Planned access involves scheduling a meeting to ensure that you'll have continued contact with power as the buying process moves forward. Suggest scheduling status meetings or biweekly standups to keep them informed—you might say, *After I meet with your team and consolidate our findings, I'd like to share the results as they relate to [BUSINESS ISSUE] we talked about today. Are Tuesdays or Thursdays best for these follow-up meetings?"* Note that the question by design doesn't allow for a simple "yes" or "no" response, but assumes the "yes" and leads the conversation in that direction.

If you're not able to negotiate planned access, an alternative strategy is conditional access, where you create the conditions under which you'll need to return for that follow-up meeting. For instance, you might ask for conditional access to the power if an unexpected issue comes up that necessitates a quick decision: *If the team survey uncovers conflicting priorities, would it be okay to contact you directly to get your perspective on how to keep this initiative moving forward?* Ultimately, whenever you're able to successfully negotiate return access upfront, you'll greatly improve your odds of riding that metaphorical elevator to the top office to continue facilitating an efficient buying process.

Speaking of negotiating, there will inevitably come a time in every buying process when you'll need to field objections and negotiate the particulars of the final deal. In the next chapter, we'll look at five proven strategies for overcoming objections and negotiating a win-win with your most demanding buyers.

12

Handling Objections and Negotiating on Value, Not Price

It's May 8 in Denver, Colorado, and Crystal wakes up to 7 inches of fresh snowfall. Last night, the temperature dropped 38 degrees in 1 hour and kept going. Of course, she knows that her home state is fond of dramatic temperature swings—still, it's a potent reminder of how fast things can change.

At 8:42 a.m. Crystal—a top-performing account executive at a video hosting company—is 18 minutes out from her fourth meeting with the head of content at a conversational intelligence (CI) company. While she knows better than to include this deal in her second quarter forecast, she's confident she can bring it home by August. After all, her company's solution is an ideal fit for the CI company's customer retention problem—the proposed video-training library will offer an improved and tailored onboarding experience, freeing up CSMs to offer more personalized experiences and address issues at the point of need. Crystal has already shored up the VisionMatch: The head of content, Rebecca, agrees that Crystal's solution is uniquely positioned to solve the problems and impact the business in a meaningful and measurable way. Like I said, things are looking good for a July/August close . . . until 5 minutes into the meeting, Rebecca says, "Look, your price is just too high."

I'm sure many of you have been here before. Dealing with objections is a core part of being in sales. Still, we don't always see it coming. When we're blindsided with a sizable objection on a crucial deal, it sets our nerves on edge; our blood pressure spikes; it's enough to throw anyone momentarily off their game. And it doesn't have to be that way.

If you take away nothing else from this chapter, internalize this: *Objections are a buying signal.* While it might feel like you're about to lose the deal, objections are typically a negotiating tactic or a cloaked request for more information. If the prospect was truly no longer interested, you wouldn't be in this situation. And if they didn't have reservations about your solution's value, the plan for implementing it or the timing, they would have already bought it. Think about it: You've already established credibility, trust, and rapport—the buyer is talking to you about their reservations, almost asking you to instill the confidence they need to buy.

This is an opportunity. Treat it as such, and you'll come out ahead.

The same goes for those tense moments in negotiation. When it comes to objection handling and negotiations, there's much overlap as well as important moments of nuance. We'll cover both in this chapter—I'll walk you through the four types of objections you'll face and a proven process for overcoming them. Then, we'll dive into five dependable tactics for negotiating a win-win with your most demanding buyers.

Understanding Objections

Instead of fleeing from objections, turn and face them with confidence.

Overcoming objections is your only pathway for moving the deal forward. If an unaddressed objection remains, the deal will never close—it's as simple as that. Welcome the opportunity to engage with the buyer where they are—whether that's in a place of doubt or a planned negotiating stance. You'll need to get them all out on the table before things progress, and to do that, you'll need to recognize the patterns and identify the common themes behind seemingly unrelated reservations. The good news is that objections typically fall into four buckets: fit, value, power, and plan/timing. Let's look at what defines each bucket and how to classify the objection you're dealing with.

Fit

You've clearly positioned your product/service as the best solution to the specific problems that make the prospect's business issue difficult to solve—and now they see things differently.

First, don't panic—many companies introduce competitors late in the process as a negotiating tactic. It might even be a functionality or feature that was dismissed in earlier conversions—the key is to go back to those earlier conversations and review the agreement on problems worth solving. Start by answering one question from the prospect's point of view: *Why does your difference matter?* Recap how your product/solution uniquely solves the problems that prevent the company from overcoming their business issue.

If you're dealing with an objection based on fit, you'll hear statements like the following:

- *It's far from ideal, but we're doing better than I expected with our current solution, so why change?*
- *Competitor X is able to provide real-time course corrections through their recommendation engine, what can your solution do in this area?*
- *There are parts I like, but I'm worried about how your solution will scale.*

Value

It's a good fit—but is it really worth it? That's the principle question your prospect has in mind if you're dealing with an objection in this area. Remember: you don't have to be the low-cost option if you're truly differentiated. However, an objection on price does mean you'll need to put in more work to uncover enough value to motivate action because there's an element missing.

When you're facing an objection based on value, you might hear statements like the following:

- *Compared to the competition, your price is significantly higher.*
- *Your solution is too expensive, and we haven't budgeted that much.*

Start by going back to the measurable value that the prospect agreed to in the first place. Remind them of the quantifiable problem and the measurable impact of your solution to investigate if things have changed. If they have, expand the conversation to see what other metrics your solution will need to impact to create the kind of value that inspires urgency. You might even acknowledge the magnitude of the expense *and* demonstrate how the value far outweighs the investment.

The impact must be measurable, time bound, and significant enough to overcome any business's innate resistance to change. As I mentioned in Chapter 3, you'll also need to win the fight for capital at the CFO level. That means going beyond ROI to showcase the organizational value of implementing your solution *and* why they should focus on this initiative rather than other competing initiatives.

It also has to be tied to the prospect's individual motivation. People do not make decisions that aren't aligned with their best interests. Without an explicit connection to the prospect's motivations, you'll fall flat every time. Now, the good news is that most B2B buyers are measured on a certain set of KPIs and rewarded accordingly, so that makes connecting to and impacting these KPIs a relatively simple task. Don't overlook the intangible side of things either. Factors like increased credibility or being perceived as a trailblazer can have a tremendous impact. When there is high personal value, people will go to the limit to see the solution carried out.

Whatever you do, promise me that you won't fall into the trap of thinking that price concessions will motivate a prospect to buy. Discounting is about as far as you can get from a cure-all—you should always defend the price in the context of the value proposition that the potential buyer has already agreed to. If you turn to discounting instead, you lose credibility and undermine the value case you spent all that time building. In the realm of complex B2B purchases, buyers who cannot clearly see—and need—the value your product/solution offers will not risk implementing it, even if it were free.

Power

Somehow, we always find ourselves back at this juncture, don't we? It goes to show how often everything comes down to one question: *Can they buy?*

When facing objections based on power, you'll likely hear something along the lines of the following:

- *I'm convinced, but this affects sales too, and I'm not in charge of that budget.*
- *Our CFO will have a lot of questions about a purchase of this size—she might not approve it.*
- *I'm not the only one affected by this solution, and I need the input of marketing too.*

Of course, things change. Maybe your initial conversations were focused on a solution that was within their decision-making authority. After uncovering additional problems, the scope of the project has gone beyond those bounds and budgets. Or perhaps, once the decision was made, you've been transferred over to the party responsible for executing that decision, i.e., procurement—and it's their objective to get the best deal possible. Whatever the reason, you now know you're not dealing with the ultimate decision-maker—flip back to Chapter 11 and gain access to the new buyer.

Plan

When dealing with objections based on the plan, the prospect may already be convinced that your solution is the ideal one—and they either have concerns over the implementation plan, or they're questioning if the timing is right.

Objections in this bucket will take forms similar to these examples:

- *I'd love to do it, but my team is too busy to implement a project of this scale.*
- *I have 9 months left on this contract with our current provider.*
- *My attention is elsewhere—can we revisit this next quarter?*

Now that you know what you're looking for, let's examine the process you'll use to address any objection and move the sale one step closer to the finish line.

Overcoming Objections

Let's check back in on Crystal—fast forward 18 months, and we find her leading a sales team who's selling into higher ed. Today, her team—along with teams from three of their fiercest competitors—is presenting to the buying committee of one of the most prestigious land-grant research universities in the country. Suffice it to say that their mascot is known as nature's ecosystem engineer and that any of the sales teams present would love to add this logo to their company's website. It also wouldn't hurt their careers if they were known as the team that made it happen.

Thanks to Crystal's connection with the buying committee lead, she's engineered it so that her team goes last. So far, so good. Now, I should mention that the size and prestige of this potential contract have already led Crystal to price this one right down to the very limit—she is coming in with their best pricing and packaging based on their needs. But that's just the icing on the cake, right? Only time will tell.

After 30 minutes, Crystal wraps up an impressive presentation that convincingly illustrates the value her solution can provide and is mapped to measurable milestones agreed upon in the mutual plan. Except, the end of the presentation is met by quizzical expressions and a very vocal member of the buying committee who's focused on one element: *price*. Luckily, Crystal knows what to do, she follows five proven steps.

Step 1: Project Confidence

Think back to Chapter 7 when we talked about the importance of going into cold calls with the right mindset—we talked about how easily a prospect can detect negative emotions like defeat, fear, or anxiety in your voice. Well, when in the boardroom delivering the final presentation, multiply that by one thousand. If you believe betraying negative emotions will affect your cold calling, you can see the potential for negative emotions wreaking sheer havoc in a situation like the one Crystal finds herself in.

That's why step one is always meeting objections with confidence. You know they're coming. Expect them; embrace them; know that this is the only path forward. This is your opportunity to learn more about your prospect's needs and opinions and communicate why they need what you're offering. When you internalize this fact, you'll view objections as a routine part of the process and a sign that you're one step closer to your goal.

Step 2: Clarify

Picking back up with Crystal, what should she do?

Should she go even lower? Should she explain how much effort her company has put in to arrive at this price to begin with? Should she immediately cut a deliverable and try to rework the cost on the spot?

Crystal knows better than to fall down any of those rabbit holes. Instead, she asks a round of clarifying questions to determine what's truly behind the buying committee member's comments on price. Guess what? Turns out, he's worried the price is too low. He remembers a purchase from 3 years ago where the initial price was extremely reasonable—then they ran into price increases 6 months later since the supplier wasn't able to keep the implementation schedule on track without additional investments. At this point, the objection isn't even about price, it's about the plan, a plan that Crystal has implemented at other universities in the past. Now, it's only a matter of defending that plan.

Bottom line: Never go further until you've clarified the other's party's position. You never know what's going on in someone's head until you ask. Often, objections take convoluted forms, and it's only after careful examination that you'll be able to determine and address the root cause. To do so, fall back on techniques you used to identify and confirm the business issues in the first place: O-P-C questions. Need a refresher? If so, go back to Chapter 6.

Step 3: Diagnose

Now, it's time to diagnose the stage in the buying process where things went out of alignment. As Crystal did previously, when she uncovered that the true motivations behind the price conversation were connected to concerns over the implementation plan and the potential for the total investment to grow, you'll need to map the objections to the Qualified Prospect Formula and find the underdeveloped component.

Think back to Chapter 9 and ask yourself some of the same questions you used to qualify the opportunity in the first place:

- **Should they buy?**
  Is your product/service effectively positioned as the unique and best solution to the specific problems that make the business issue difficult to solve?
- **Is it worth it?**
  After considering all of the effort that goes into implementing complex solutions like time/money spent, departmental priorities, organizational culture, and competing initiatives—has the customer confirmed that the quantifiable impact of moving forward is enough to justify the expense?
- **When will they buy?**
  Do you have a mutually agreed-upon timeline that includes milestones and specificity on what has to happen before, during, and after the purchase to realize the promised value? Remember: You must focus buyers on the future results and value realization—the timeline you've crafted with them is simply the roadmap. Are they confident in it?

Step 4: Sharp Angle Close

If the objection you're fielding is a negotiating tactic in disguise, this is how you'll surface all the remaining objections all at once. The sharp angle close is summed up by this question: *If we come to an agreement on (value, plan, etc.) is there anything else that could stop you from moving forward?*

Once you identify all of the barriers, it places you in a stronger position because with all of the objections on the table, you can formulate a strategy to address them in totality. You can change the terms, functionality, deliverables, or other elements of the buying equation to add more value—but you'll struggle to do so if you don't expand the conversation at this point.

Step 5: Address

Here's the big secret: sometimes addressing the objection itself is the simplest part. Once you've clarified the objection, diagnosed the underlying condition, and surfaced any hidden agendas and lingering confusion, the path to marking this deal closed-won will emerge. After all, things change—constantly. Even toward the end of the buying process, you might find yourself needing to further educate, clarify, or defend, and that's fine—if you expect it.

Ultimately, most buying processes end with some form of negotiation, so let's turn our attention to this vital skillset.

Negotiating Like a Chief Procurement Officer

Negotiations are no picnic—even for the rainmakers.

The mere mention of the word likely conjures an image of an executive sitting on the other side of a boardroom table with an expression that's almost daring you to challenge them, or a ring light shining in your eyes while you try to nonchalantly search through the negotiating prompts that you've written out on sticky notes in a halo surrounding your computer monitor. They're stressful events that test your nerve, your rapport with prospects, and reveal points of misalignment in the buying cycle—and it's common for sales orgs to invest heavily in helping sellers hold their ground.

I still remember my first training on negotiating. Shuffling into the Marriott conference room, expecting the typical slow-roll start while everyone gets settled—only to be hit with a wall of energy. My company hired a phenomenal negotiator to put us through a rigorous 1-day training. It was about as far from the much-overused lecture style of training as you can get—not only was he engaging, he was practically a stand-up comic who had us laughing all day. We had small seminar-style sessions, roleplays, and one-on-one coaching from the facilitator—and more roleplays. I left thoroughly exhausted, yet eager to apply what I'd learned—feeling like I'd gone up against one of the masters and held my ground, I was on top of the world and ready to meet any negotiation challenge with poise and confidence . . . then I learned that the procurement team at my largest potential client had gone through the same training. Two full weeks of the same training compared to my 1 day!

Make no mistake—that's what you're up against. While negotiating is a part of your job, you're going against individuals for which negotiating *is* their job—let's help you prepare by looking at a five-step process that has served me well.

Step 1: Choose Your Moment

If the prospect so much as furrows his brow, the salesperson starts piling on embellishments and discounts. The salesperson starts negotiating at the first sign of hesitation—before the buyer has truly been sold on her solution. While it sounds incredible, this is the number one mistake sellers make. If you're not talking to power and haven't connected your solution to problems worth solving right now, there's no magical mix of embellishments and discounts that will propel the deal to close.

Taking this approach will turn the sale into a product-focused process—in turn, your solution will be viewed as a commodity, and the chief differentiator becomes price. Instead of incentivizing quick action, you undermine your credibility, compromise price integrity, and put yourself at a tremendous disadvantage.

The next step is to draw a line separating the negotiator from the negotiating tactic: *Don't take it personally*. This includes preparing yourself to take the buyer's initial negative response in stride. Remember, your job is to acknowledge the buyer's position, ensure they feel heard, and gather as much information as possible to gain a holistic view of their position.

Finally, don't forget to go into every negotiation knowing your leverage points—by reviewing earlier conversations and the case for justifying the purchase, you'll uncover the points that piqued the prospect's interest in the first place and can use these to your advantage. Pay special attention to things like your track record, your technology, performance, pricing, or CX.

Step 2: Know What's Negotiable

First things first: Ensure you know if your organization has any "showstoppers." If they exist, find ways to communicate them early in the buying process. Next, you'll need to understand the extent of your negotiating authority.

Every company has negotiables and nonnegotiables. What you're empowered to negotiate and what needs to be escalated varies tremendously from organization to organization.

Many companies I work with use an "empowerment matrix." This tool breaks down deals by size and shows the level of authority that different roles might have to deviate from the standard arrangement. For example, for deals of $150K–250K, sellers might be able to offer a 5% discount and for certain embellishments, managers can give 7% and other embellishments—anything else is escalated to the vice president level. As I mentioned, these terms vary greatly, so knowing what your company expects is critical.

Remember to never negotiate on a single element—all three dimensions are interconnected, and elements of all can go into your final negotiating strategy. As you can see in Figure 12.1, terms and conditions and deliverables come first. Begin the negotiating process with these elements—price is always a function of the other two variables.

Collaborating to find creative ways to create joint value should always be your go-to move. However, if you overstep and have to retract an element of your new proposal, you risk seriously damaging the credibility, trust, and rapport you've painstakingly built with the potential buyer. Strategize with your manager beforehand to ensure you understand all the options, and all forms those options can take.

NegotiationPrompter®

	Prospect's Ideal Solution	Your Ideal Solution	Strategy
Terms & Conditions			
Deliverables			
Price			

Figure 12.1 NegotiationPrompter®.
Source: Adapted from ValueSelling Associates.

Step 3: Make a Trade

Okay, the deck has been dealt, and you know every permutation of every bargaining chip at your disposal—time to look at the tools you'll use to ensure it ends with everyone holding a winning hand.

The first tool at your disposal is the trade-off. This is a negotiating tactic that trades one item in one of the three categories for something else in the other two categories. For instance, I may give a concession on billing terms to maintain price, or I might meet your price discount in exchange for a customer testimonial. To execute on this, carefully listen to the buyer's concerns, identify areas of flexibility, and get creative where you can. For instance, you might not be able to install your product in the 30-day timeline the buyer is asking for, but you can make the trade to extend the license for 3 extra months. Or perhaps, you get the sense that year-end dollars are precious— offer more compelling payment terms that rely on a small initial investment and push the bulk of the spend into the first and second quarters. It's also common that year-end budgets need to be used. In that case, a discount might be back on the table if the client prepays for services.

Step 4: Sweeten the Deal

The next tool to throw into the mix is embellishments—these are your high-value, low-cost deliverables that you can use to maintain price integrity. Here you're adding an item in one category to maintain stability in the other categories.

If your company hosts an industry event like the Sales Enablement Summit, Gartner CSO & Sales Leader Conference, or Dreamforce, including complimentary passes is a phenomenal tactic. If you sell a XaaS (anything as a service) solution, another proven tactic is offering additional training hours or user seats if applicable. The key here is to review your discovery notes—what caught their interest early on that you've lost sight of? Was there a feature or add-on they considered in the beginning that was ultimately sacrificed due to budget? You get the idea. The better you know the prospect's unique business and desires, the better luck you'll have adding on embellishments that add both personal and professional value and allow you to keep the price the same and add more value.

Step 5: Compromise

It's inevitable—sometimes you simply have to compromise. Once you've isolated the underlying issue—whether it's tied to deliverables, terms and conditions, or price—find the middle ground that will satisfy you and the prospect. The trick to compromise is to focus the discussion on a single category. You must diagnose, isolate, and confirm—then make your offer.

■ ■ ■

In the end, objection handling and negotiating rely on one thing: your understanding of the value you can bring to customers.

Success comes to those who invest the time upfront to investigate and understand the professional and personal value that their prospects are seeking. The foundation of any negotiation is agreed-upon value—have the price conversation before reaching a consensus on value and you put yourself at a terrible disadvantage. Only after developing a robust understanding of the customer's business and the value they expect to receive are you in a position to defend the price. No matter your industry, product, or experience level, these tactics have served me well over my more than 25 years in sales. I'm confident they'll help you close more business as well.

V

Cement Customer Relationships

13

Land and Expand: Strategies for Account Penetration

My first field sales job was as an account manager—despite its widespread status today, the role was unique for my employer at the time.

All the field reps at the time covered a specific geographic area, a *large* geo-specific area. My peers had territories like the entirety of New England and were calling on companies over a six-state area. Others had smaller territories by comparison, covering a single state—for example, all businesses in Michigan or Ohio.

In contrast, my territory was not six states, but six named accounts. My objective was to grow our revenue in those accounts and those accounts only. I carried a $600K quota—and while that might not seem like a lot, it quickly becomes challenging when you're working with an average deal size of $10K. To accomplish this goal, I knew I needed to formulate a plan that would enable me to hit my number. The good news was these were large computer vendors I was selling into—Digital Equipment Corporation (DEC) and Data General, for example, and I had 1 year to do it. I knew I needed a focused plan—the bad news was I didn't know where to start or how to attack my goal. And as we'll examine in this chapter, starting off with a strategy that directs where you'll spend your energies is vital to your future success.

■ ■ ■

The concept of a land-and-expand strategy is simple on the surface: By closing a small piece of business in an account, you are then able to expand your footprint by creating and closing more across the organization.

The strategy, too, is straightforward. If we can delight our customers, it's a logical conclusion they will want to continue—and increase—the amount of business they do with us. Plus, the subsequent sale should be faster. We're an established vendor they've bought from before; procurement/vendor management knows how to work with us; we have agreed upon terms and conditions for working together; and the fundamental negotiations have already taken place.

We have access. We have relationships, and they have a vested interest in meeting with us and to continue exploring avenues for adding value between the two organizations. And if they're happy with our products/services, it's reasonable to assume they'll be happy with additional products and services that we have to offer.

What could go wrong?

■ ■ ■

While it might seem like you're working with a tremendous advantage, good account planning never happens by accident.

The challenge for most account managers in the aforementioned situation is to identify how to best focus on high-potential opportunities and avoid having their attention diffused. Creating a focused plan becomes critical for execution, time, and priority management. In addition, the account manager is typically working as part of a geographically distributed team to execute the land-and-expand strategy.

For example, when I was an account manager, I managed the relationships with our client at their headquarters locations. While many purchase decisions were made and executed through headquarters and the teams I worked with, there was also a distributed component to their organization. They had geographic regions with autonomous decision-making power and additional business units that were located outside of headquarters.

Because of the makeup of our client organizations, our coverage model was also distributed. I was partnering with sales professionals in those remote regions and business units to grow the business. I had the responsibility of communicating with them and influencing their behavior to successfully create and close opportunities.

This is the situation many account managers still find themselves in. Not only do you have to have a plan, but I had to communicate that plan, secure buy-in from peers across the globe, and keep everyone focused on the ultimate goal of growing the account revenue while there are a thousand other pressing issues competing for their attention.

With that in mind, let's look at the two strategies you'll use to maximize the potential of key accounts—upsell and cross-sell—and walk through the steps you'll take to execute them.

Upsell. The sales professional creates an opportunity to sell more of what they initially sold to the same buyer. The first sale may be to provide a software license to 100 users or employees. The upsell is to sell another 100 users or licenses to the same company. In this instance, the decision-maker is the same; the buying process is the same; and the sales rep is familiar with the buyer's decision-making process.

Cross-Sell. There are two kinds of cross-sell strategies. The first is when sales reps identify new buyers in the account to sell the same products and services to. For instance, if I've installed my product/service in the North American geographic organization, I can then create winnable opportunities for similar geographic regions in Europe, Asia, South America, and the other theaters where the business operates.

The second type of cross-sell begins with identifying new products, services, or solutions that I can sell into the installed business unit. If the client has purchased our sales methodology for their field sales, I can create winnable opportunities for them to also implement our account planning programs or business development programs for the same teams of people.

Getting Started

The first key to any successful account expansion strategy is always research.

To identify where you can create additional opportunities, you have to begin with a complete understanding of each account and how its organized. In earlier chapters, we addressed the importance and mechanics of thoroughly researching organizations and individuals. When your aim is to expand your business in a single account, the fundamental understanding of those accounts becomes even more critical.

Key components of account planning research include the following:

- What business are they in?
- What markets are they operating in?
- What is driving their market today? Is it growing and expanding, steady, or in decline?
- Are their industry trends impacting their business?
- What are the opportunities and threats to the industry or their business?

In addition, understanding the financials and organization of the account at a high level is equally important:

- Are they profitable?
- What are the trends over the past 2 to 3 years?
- Have they had any significant mergers or acquisitions? Divestitures?
- How are they organized? Who are the key executives of the firm?
- Who are the likely executives or managers who would be interested in your offering?

While these are key pieces of knowledge that any sales rep would want to understand for their accounts, when you're focusing on only one account, it becomes even more imperative to further develop your high-level understanding of these elements and dig deep.

Armed with this information, you can begin to plot the targets for business development within the account. Do this with the aid of a white space analysis—the process of mapping the organization of an account to the products and services you offer. It can be as simple as an Excel spreadsheet where the rows denote your products/services and the columns represent other regions or business units of the account.

The "white space" shows a high-level overview of your opportunities for expansion. As you can see in Figure 13.1, opportunities can be identified by geography, and depending on the organization of the account, you can do a similar analysis of the account by business unit. While this is a basic example, the exercise can get as granular as necessary to visually identify the areas where you haven't sold your products and to create opportunities and increase the revenue you'll earn from the account.

Armed with the white space analysis and your newfound knowledge of the company's inner workings and financial health, you can move to identify the executives, managers, and decision-makers who would likely be involved in a decision to purchase and install your products and services.

	Sales Offering	Marketing Offering	Customer Service Offering
North America	*Installed*		*Installed*
EMEA			
LATAM		*Installed*	
APAC			*Installed*

Figure 13.1   High-level White Space Analysis by Geography.

Competitive Landscape

The next foundational element you'll need to examine is the competitive landscape for your accounts.

Similar to the white space analysis, you can identify where the competition is installed. For certain products and services, you may be able to identify the expiration dates of existing contracts. In turn, this helps you understand the windows of opportunity, maximize your selling time, and create a strategy to displace the competition. Any effective competitive strategy will include education, creating contrast between the installed supplier and yourself, and finding a successful differentiator while adding incremental value.

Leveraging Your Relationships

I learned early on in my account management career that when I'm introduced internally, the time to engage a new buyer in an existing account is much shorter.

Make no mistake: Prospecting in existing accounts is still prospecting. Yet, you have the distinct advantage of preexisting relationships. As the white space analysis unfolds, ensure you know the business professionals who are responsible for the problems you can solve in the expanded account view.

As with all prospecting, you're going to "campaign" to gain access to those individuals—your campaign is founded on providing value-added interruptions through targeted content and insight that is purposefully designed to intrigue and engage the new prospects. One tactic that has served me well over the years is leveraging the current relationships in a given account as springboards to new ones: Who can they introduce you to? Who can they invite to join your next meeting?

For instance, I once approached a current client and asked if we could share our success with her colleagues. She had a standing monthly meeting with her peers from various business units around the globe. Together we created a short webinar where she shared her experience and introduced me to the audience. I was prepared—not with a sales pitch—but with insights on a current issue everyone in their industry was facing.

The result was outstanding. The successful presentation paved the way for me to follow up and reach out for a conversation with key prospects. And my client's peers appreciated that she introduced them to a valuable resource. The short-term result was a number of new opportunities created in our land-and-expand strategy. The long-term result was that over the subsequent 6 months, 75% of these converted to revenue and closed-won business for my company.

A second way to leverage your relationships is to understand who you're connected with. According to the U.S. Department of Labor, 30% of the total workforce will now change jobs every 12 months.[1] It stands to reason that the networks of colleagues that today's sales professionals will create over time will be larger than they have ever been. And with data like the aforementioned stat, opportunities for introductions inside target accounts will follow suit. Mining your network for connections to new buyers is a terrific way to identify someone who can introduce you and warm that prospect up for your call.

■ ■ ■

With your white space analysis in place, competitive installations pinpointed and likely target buyers identified, you're now in an excellent position to create expansion business opportunities—provided you sidestep one common pitfall.

In my experience, sales reps working existing account opportunities don't apply the same process and rigor to these opportunities as they would to a new business opportunity. Remember: Success with one solution or success in one business unit is not a guarantee of future success. It is the foundation you must build upon.

After all, when a client is satisfied with one of your products or services, they often want more and more—and when you have multiple product lines that can be sold to the same potential buyer, your expansion program enables your success.

For example, my company, ValueSelling Associates, has a flagship program that we're known as a leader in our industry for. Several years ago, many of our long-term clients weren't even aware that we had additional programs to offer! Yes, shame on us for not doing a better job of marketing and communicating our additional offerings. However, the reality is that until someone has a specific need they can connect to you, many good messages and products/services become white noise and are ignored.

Upon realizing this, we changed our tactics. We changed our conversations. The impact was a bigger pipeline for the newer and less-known programs. The process is simple—one that you can apply regardless of your industry or what you're selling: Stop talking about the solution and begin talking about the problem that the solution addresses—take our own medicine and begin to drink our own champagne.

Ultimately, creating new opportunities with existing buyers can't be a product- or solution-led process. When it is, the customer will likely say: *Thank you; that's interesting, and I'm all set right now*. Rather, you must initiate the conversation by discussing the additional problems you can solve and the incremental value this will add. Any new opportunity for your solution will always begin with a problem—a problem worth solving that's confirmed between you and your prospect.

14

Creating Brand Advocates and Customers for Life

Devon is in his third year as an account executive at a mid-size CRM company—he enjoys the work, his coworkers, the culture, and the workflows that help him stay on track and balance the demands of filling the pipeline, maintaining the pipeline, and retaining current customers. Whether he's walking through light snow in the winter with the heavily salted streets crunching under his Chelsea boots or cruising along the canal on his bike in spring, the sight of his company's logo as he rounds the corner onto Third St. is always a welcome sight. Sure, he has his good and bad days like the rest of us, but almost every day he arrives at work energized and hopeful.

What makes it such a good fit?

As the former power forward on his college basketball team with a degree in organizational psychology, Devon thrives in the fast-paced, structured, and team-oriented environment that this CRM company provides—not to mention the playbooks. This company has a playbook for *everything*. There's a playbook for constructing sales cadences, cold-calling, onboarding new customers, monitoring platform usage, and, of course, one for renewing contracts.

Don't worry—as usual, Devon is on it. When he sold this account last September, he set the alert in his CRM for a 6-month check-in and one for a month out from renewal. The 6-month meeting went well. The client had absolutely zero complaints, and the system showed that all 20 user seats were active on a weekly basis. After all, they only submitted one, *just one*, troubleshooting ticket in their first 6 months of use—this is a testament to how skilled Devon is at following through on all the steps laid out in that dense onboarding playbook. Today is the day of the final check-in before contract renewal—Devon has a 10:30 a.m. meeting with the vice president of sales he sold to last year, and he's already going the extra mile. He's double-checked his dashboards on usage stats, did a quick scan for any company news he may have missed, and even contacted his colleagues in support to ensure there are no outstanding tech issues associated with this account. At 10:30 a.m. on the dot, the vice president joins the call and enthusiastically greets Devon. They catch up on small talk: the weather, the latest gastropub to open downtown, the gossip surrounding the upcoming NCAA basketball season. As soon as they're past the pleasantries, the client vice president brings the hammer down—they've already signed with a competitor. They'll use this last month to move their data and that's that.

Devon is understandably flabbergasted—he brings up the usage numbers, the lack of support tickets, the conversation they had 5 months earlier. The vice president agrees on all counts—they have been actively using the platform, there have been minimal tech hiccups, and they did have a good conversation 6 months back. There were no issues at that time. But guess what? *Things changed.*

Despite his best efforts and his focus on following company playbooks and protocols to the letter, Devon fails to secure the renewal. Because he was set up to fail. Because his company's protocols led him to make the cardinal mistake of renewal sales: *He conflated using a solution with receiving value from a solution.*

■ ■ ■

The scale of the customer-retention problem—and the benefits of getting it right—are sizable enough to capture the attention of any executive:

- Ninety-six percent of your customers will leave over a poor customer experience.[1]
- Increasing customer retention by 5% can lead to a profit increase ranging from 25% to 95%.[2]
- Of B2B companies, 62% don't have targets for "closing the loop" on negative customer feedback and are generally the slowest to act.[3]
- A well-engineered customer success program can yield a 91% ROI over the course of 3 years.[4]
- Eighty percent of organizations expect to compete primarily on CX.[5]
- Forty-four percent of organizations focus more on acquiring customers, while only 18% focus on retaining customers.[6]

With numbers like that, it's shocking that so many of the companies I work with seem to take renewal sales for granted. The problem is many of us are still prone to "hit-and-run" selling. Sellers secure the order, and then disappear until the renewal is due. The truth is that customer retention begins during the sales process, before the customer is won. Reinforcing, communicating, and reviewing the purchase decision throughout the relationship will help to solidify the business relationship over time.

While it's true that having initially won the business might give you a leg up, renewals are never guaranteed. And yet, their value to the business is unquestionable. A key aspect of your role as a salesperson is to maintain and grow the revenue from your existing customers. When you lose a customer, you've lost a key corporate asset. It costs many times more to acquire a new customer than to maintain an existing one, which is why the most profitable business relationships are long-lasting ones. Not only is it the foundation of any company's recurring revenue stream and stability, but it's also the best path toward realizing higher customer lifetime value and generating long-lasting customer loyalty.

It's not surprising that high-performing revenue teams learned long ago that successful customer retention efforts start with a seamless onboarding experience, expectation-setting, and a clear path to value realization. They stay in touch with everyone involved in the purchase decision throughout the life cycle of the relationship, reinforce buying decisions, uncover new needs, and are accountable for deliverables and services from the end user to the ultimate decision-maker. Top performers also make a habit of extending their activities well beyond the signed purchase order—they follow the mutual plan through the implementation process, monitoring along the way, ensuring they hit those key milestones where value is realized and confirming its impact.

To enable this process, sellers must treat existing customers with the same attention and dedication they show to new prospects if they want to build brand advocates and create customers for life. Each renewal cycle and every interaction therein is your opportunity to identify new ways to deliver value and give the customer a reason to stay. In this chapter, I'll break down the four-step process I've used throughout my career to jump-start renewal sales and build customer loyalty, before touching on how sales leaders can extend these principles to the entire revenue engine.

Step 1: Demonstrating Your Commitment to Customer Success

What have you done to add value to a key customer this week?

It's a simple question, and at the same time, it can feel like an impossible ask. Between filling the pipeline, managing the pipeline, and working with clients to realize results, it feels like we have absolutely no time to spend coddling the customers who have already bought our products or solutions—yet engaging with clients through regular, value-added interactions is the primary mechanism for building customer loyalty. The question becomes: *How can you turn activities that are already in your daily, selling workflows into activities that generate value for existing clients?*

Let's say you've already signed SkyLabs—it was a fantastic fit, and you're looking to replicate your success. You've started researching their competitors, and Nebula Engineering looks promising, so you've set up alerts in LinkedIn Sales Navigator for newsworthy events. This morning, you're pinged with the news that Nebula Engineering acquired another company to expand its offerings. Not only will this information give you a leg up in your outreach efforts, but it's also vital industry intel that your contacts at SkyLabs may not have seen yet. Immediately, bringing it to the attention of your contact at SkyLabs is a low-effort way to add value that fits neatly into your prospecting research.

This is merely one example, but you get the idea—small, personalized interactions across regular intervals are the key to staying top-of-mind and hooked into what's happening at your client companies.

Checking in from time to time demonstrates to customers that you see them as more than a series of commission checks—it justifies the trust they put in you in the first place and sets you up for a successful second or third sale because you've made the process of buying from you a lower risk proposition. Another benefit of regular contact is the window it provides into the organization, what's changing: People move; responsibilities shift; product needs will evolve. Use these opportunities for proactive communication: reviewing business issues and uncovering new problems that you are uniquely positioned to address with your solutions.

Step 2: Identifying Why Customers Leave

I'm sure you've heard it too:

Well, the way we do things here is different.
We're unique in the way that we handle x, y, and z.
We're anything but traditional; we're focused on a novel way of doing business that . . .

Every company, prospect, and customer will have no problem rattling off numerous examples of how their business, needs, and goals are different. As sales professionals, we know that challenges, needs, and goals tend to be eerily similar once you get to the heart of the matter—the same goes for customer retention.

Perhaps, the handoff from sales to customer success didn't go as planned, and rapport was damaged by asking the customer to clarify goals—the same could happen in handoffs between account executives or when bringing in SMEs to solve and explain technical issues. Or maybe, they didn't receive the value they expected in the time promised. It could also be something completely outside of your control like a power shift within the client organization. The key is to monitor potential red flags like these and to reach out immediately when you see something. Not sure where to start? Begin by running through the following checklist.

Common areas for improvement:

- Regular, value-added customer interactions and check-ins
- Closing the loop on negative feedback
- Providing quick solutions to issues with implementation

- Ensuring all customer-facing roles have the tools to efficiently understand the client's business issues and path to value realization
- Being prepared to add value and learn more with every interaction

Step 3: Leaning into Your Data

Devon showed us why you should never conflate product/solution usage with receiving value—yet, there's still tremendous insight to be gained by investigating *how* your customers are using your solution: Do they gravitate toward a certain feature set? Are they leveraging reporting appropriately to monitor impact? Is there an underutilized part of your solution that has the potential to align more closely with the latest business issues?

Put on your analyst hat and dive into the data that is available to you. You can look for patterns in usage data, examine what marketing collateral they're engaging with, and research market trends. The idea is to come to the table with an understanding of the new challenges that are likely top-of-mind for your customers. Going back to Devon, he may have been able to save the account if he'd dug into the usage data and saw that user alerts weren't properly tailored to the company's selling process. Unfortunately, without crucial knowledge like this, he was at a phenomenal disadvantage from the start.

Step 4: Uncovering New Problems

Of course, the exact opposite of the previous can happen—and ideally, it does. Your solutions were the fix for the client's most-pressing business issue.

Tremendous . . . except, now what happens?

Time to give the customer a reason to stay—that means going back to the beginning and applying the same process and rigor that you used to win the opportunity in the first place. It's as simple as going back to your questioning process that I covered in Chapter 6 and requalifying the opportunity from the prospect's point of view as we talked about in Chapter 9. It all comes down to similar questions, with slight tweaks in areas of focus.

Are You Differentiated?

Does the customer believe your solutions will continue to measurably impact their unique business issue? If you're selling into a new part of the business or providing a different type of solution, ask: Why is your solution the ideal one in the prospect's mind?

What's in It for Them?

Ideally, the buyer already received the impact they were seeking from the initial solution and implementation—now it's time to understand new needs and align to them. Buyers will always crave trusted advisors and make rational decisions for emotional reasons. Personal value is particularly important when it comes to customer retention and ongoing loyalty.

Can They Buy Again?

Budgets are shifted; departments are consolidated; authority levels change in times of increased economic uncertainty. You might have sold into a buying group of seven last time—now it's a buying group of 12. Last year, you sold to the head of marketing, which was fine when they reported to the CEO—now both the sales and marketing lead report to a new CRO. If you want a long-lasting relationship with that organization, you'll need to engage within the altered power structure and bring the CRO on board.

Do They Believe in the ROI?

There's always another option—including going back to the former status quo. Last year, you provided them with a compelling case to change—now you need to give them an equally compelling reason for them to stay.

Review your first discovery conversations, the latest usage data, and notes from all of your check-ins. What's changed? What did you not anticipate? What can you learn? Was something missed? Ensure your new plan to deliver value is impactful and qualified at both the company and individual level.

Remember: Past value will not motivate future behavior.

When Things Go Wrong

In spite of flawless onboarding and communication, sometimes things don't go as planned. Eventually, it's inevitable, and it will happen to all of us.

The good news is customers don't expect perfection—they expect responsiveness; they want to be seen and heard. How you handle that is critically important.

Over the years, I've learned to maximize my time with simple strategies for both preventing and restoring a relationship when things go sideways. Let's look at prevention first.

1. Communicate in writing and confirm agreements.

    We're all busy, and our customers are no different. They leave our meetings with barely a moment to take a breath and often forget the commitments, timelines, or agreements that were made verbally. When you confirm all relevant details back to a customer in a written summary, not only does it help avoid any misunderstanding, it's often greatly appreciated by busy executives or managers.

2. Avoid assumptions.

I was once told, "I assume that you knew that training was not included in the software purchase." *What? Why would anyone assume that?* I was buying a solution, and I expected my investment to cover a successful implementation. I was wrong—it goes to show how quickly assumptions can become the root cause of a deal-breaking problem or nagging issue.

3. Be honest and upfront.

I often have the opportunity to speak with our clients early in their buying journey. Sometimes they know exactly what they want. Other times, they aren't quite sure. There have been times when I've told a potential client that we're not the best fit for them because I don't want to be the hit-and-run sales professional or advisor who takes the deal and sacrifices my reputation. Every B2B buyer would rather work with someone who is upfront and transparent than a slick sales professional who only tells them what they want to hear in order to win the opportunity.

4. Accountability.

Let's face it—regardless of your role in the revenue engine, you're the face of your company in your client's eyes. Dependable and thorough follow-up is a crucial component of accountability and relationship building: You must do what you said you will do—and if you can't meet those expectations, it's time to proactively set timelines and expectations. Accountability also means owning up when things go wrong *and* demonstrating to clients that you're growing from experiences that aren't as positive as everyone would like.

5. Add value.

We become memorable when we delight customers and bring unexpected value that impacts their lives and professional experiences. Every conversation should have a purpose and the capacity to make a positive difference. The check-in call shouldn't be merely for you to ask, *How's it going?* It should be an opportunity to share an insight, idea or best practice that makes a difference for the client. A former manager of mine taught me to always have a "goodie" to share with my clients. He didn't mean a gift, trinket, or branded swag—he meant a value-added insight that would contribute to building a customer for life.

Now, let's examine restorative strategies to use when your customers are frustrated or dissatisfied.

1. Back up and start over.

    I recently had a client escalate a situation to my attention. She was upset, *really* upset. The root cause of her frustration was clearly a misunderstanding on her part. Yet, I've never been successful at telling a client that they may be wrong—and I certainly don't recommend that approach. Instead, I asked to start over, *With your permission, may we rewind this to reset the relationship and our go-forward strategy?* Sometimes, it's as simple as that—with that agreement in place, she could vent, and I could listen. Then, we reframed the situation and formed a new strategy collaboratively.

2. Leverage the positive.

    The worst thing that can happen when something goes wrong is the customer doesn't let you know—instead of initiating a difficult conversation, they ghost you. When we have the opportunity to communicate, that fact in and of itself is a positive. Focus on celebrating that you have an opportunity to address the issue in the first place. Then, find the good—typically, not everything breaks at once. How can you leverage what's working to help counteract the negative?

3. Take responsibility.

    Just as accountability is a key tactic to avoid a customer problem, responsibility is the crucial factor in resolving the problem when it arises. Responsibility increases trust and provides an opportunity to learn and improve. Use the problem as a path for improvement. While negative feedback is often difficult to hear, it's like oxygen to your revenue engine business. Celebrate the customers who have the courage to share their dissatisfaction and use that as fuel to improve in the future.

4. Be proactive.

Always deliver bad news before the storm than after it. When you have a difficult message to deliver, the sooner the better. Delaying and denying the impact on our customers never improves the situation—it often makes it worse by shortening their timeline to act. Remember: Difficult messages are always best delivered in person or via a phone call, not as a surprise email or text—or worse yet, a press release to the general public. As revenue professionals, difficult messages should not be a surprise for our customers.

5. Develop a mutual plan.

As I mentioned in step 3, customers who are willing to share their dissatisfaction are a blessing—now it's time to use that as fuel for future growth. Develop a collaborative plan that includes time-bound milestones for getting things back on track. This isn't about how you'll get from a 5 to a 10 on the customer satisfaction scale—ask them what you'll need to do to hit 15.

Creating a Consistent CX Across the Entire Revenue Engine

For the most part, the aforementioned examples address the situation where the sales professional is responsible for maintaining existing customers and securing new ones, or a setup where they work very closely with their counterpart on the renewal side of the business. As we discussed way back in Chapter 1, some revenue teams are moving away from this approach—instead, they have specialized sellers with hard lines of responsibility for different parts of the buying process. When this is the case, any organization that has a vested interest in delivering the most value to customers—not to mention improving customer lifetime value—will enable information to be readily available and digestible regardless of where an individual sits in the revenue engine.

I know, easier said than done. The reality in most large sales organizations plays out differently. You might have consistency across an SDR team or your account executive team across the western United States—but things look very different inside the European teams or the enterprise team handling the US East Coast territories, and customer success might as well live on a whole different planet! In this alarmingly common scenario, how do you decide what good looks like? And who decides? You can't leave it up to the individual sales teams, or else you'd wind up with no chance of scaling success, when and if you find it.

As I mentioned in Chapter 9, the true power of the approach I've outlined in this book lies in its application across the entire revenue engine and its impact on the overall CX. When your entire organization adopts a common language, framework, and set of tools, vital information is efficiently transferred between all customer-facing roles. That means seamless handoffs between sales and customer success, where CSMs can be quickly brought up to speed on the value the customer expects to receive and the agreed-upon roadmap for arriving there. The same is true for other SMEs that need to be pulled in from across the organization—even if they've never made a single sales call, this shared framework enables them to understand the client's business issues and goals and work to help them achieve meaningful results. As humans, we seek stability and dependability. It's the foundation of trust, and trust is the foundation of any long-lasting relationship. When you create a consistent CX across the entire customer life cycle, you build brand advocates and customers for life. *How you sell is as important as what you sell.*

■ ■ ■

In the end, every business relationship, every buying process, every sales call depends on one question: *Is it worth it?*

Value is how people justify spending their time and justifying the expenditure to purchase—and as I've touched on at several points in this book, *it's personal*. Everyone makes buying decisions based on their unique experiences and perspective. Each and every one of those decisions is unique—but that doesn't mean we can't apply the same framework and process to all of them.

For as long as there has been commerce, there have been buyers and sellers. I'm confident that will not change. As Todd Caponi mentioned in his Foreword, thought leaders have been prophesizing the death of the salesperson since at least 1912—and it's likely that these predictions have been around since the first recorded sales transaction. From Thomas Herbert Russell's 1912 reaction to catalogs and advertisements to Forrester's infamous 2015 *Death of a (B2B) Salesman* report to Gartner's latest finding that 72% of customers prefer a rep-free experience,[7] one thing remains: the sales professional. And that will not change for strategic B2B buying.

If sales professionals are focused on forging human-to-human connections built on delivering value in every interaction, they become more than a seller—they become a trusted advisor who provides confidence in high-stakes buying decisions. I don't know about you, but if my career was potentially on the line over a purchasing decision, all of the AI-generated feedback in the world would do nothing to alleviate my anxiety. I'd turn to a trusted business advisor, a friend. As I recounted in Chapter 2, at my friend Dan's funeral, his CEO said, "What made Dan so effective was that he never tried to turn his friends into clients. Instead, he turned every client into a friend." That's the kind of sales professional I'd turn to, and that's the kind of sales professional you will be when you put these principles into practice.

As always, sell on value.

— Julie Thomas

Notes

Foreword

1. Gartner. (n.d.). *Gartner says adaptable sales organizations must rethink their customer understanding, engagement and operating models* [online]. Available at: https://www.gartner.com/en/newsroom/press-releases/2022-05-17-gartner-says-adaptable-sales-organizations-must-rethink-ther-customer-understanding-engagement-and-operating-models.
2. Forrester. (n.d.). *One million B2B sales jobs eliminated by 2020* [online]. Available at: https://www.forrester.com/press-newsroom/one-million-b2b-sales-jobs-eliminated-by-2020/ [Accessed 5 May 2023].

Chapter 1

1. Turner, J. (2022). *7 technology disruptions that will completely change sales[online]*. Gartner. Available at: https://www.gartner.com/en/articles/7-technology-disruptions-that-will-completely-change-sales.
2. Gotlieb, D. and Rosenberg, C. (2022). *115 reasons to attend the sales tech mayhem after-party* [online]. Gartner. Available at: https://blogs.gartner.com/dan-gottlieb/2022/07/20/115-reasons-to-attend-the-sales-tech-mayhem-after-party/.
3. Lusha. (2022). *The state of b2b sales 2022* [online]. Available at: https://campaigns.lusha.com/infographics/infographics-data-report.
4. Gartner. (2022). *Gartner says adaptable sales organizations must rethink their customer understanding, engagement and operating models* [online]. Press release. Available at: https://www.gartner.com/en/newsroom/press-releases/2022-05-17-gartner-says-adaptable-sales-organizations-must-rethink-ther-customer-understanding-engagement-and-operating-models.
5. Bruce, I. and Pregler, M. (2022). *B2B sellers must reevalute how they build trust with buyers* [online]. Forrester. Available at: https://www.forrester.com/blogs/b2b-sellers-must-reevaluate-how-they-build-trust-with-buyers/.

6. Shea, M. (n.d.). *Today's buyers want insight, guidance, and efficiencies* [online]. SellingPower. Available at: https://www.sellingpower.com/20133/todays-buyers-want-insights-guidance-and-efficiencies.

7. Sherrard, S., Dave, R., and MacGregor, M.P. (2022). What b2bs need to know about their buyers. *Harvard Business Review*. Available at: https://hbr.org/2022/09/what-b2bs-need-to-know-about-their-buyers?trk=lss-blog-brand-outreach-hurt-brand.

8. Gartner. (n.d.). *The b2b buying journey* [online]. Available at: https://www.gartner.com/en/sales/insights/b2b-buying-journey.

Chapter 2

1. Shea, M. (2022). *Out with the old and in with the new: Millennials upend B2B sales* [online]. Outreach (13 July). Available at: https://www.outreach.io/resources/blog/millennials-upend-b2b-sales.

2. Newport, C. (2016). *Deep work: Rules for focused success in a distracted world.* Hachette UK.

Chapter 3

1. Blum, K. (2021). *Gartner keynote: B2B sales must focus on seller-assisted digital experiences* [online]. Garter. Available at: https://www.gartner.com/smarterwithgartner/b2b-sales-must-focus-on-seller-assisted-digital-experiences.

2. Bruce, I. (2021). *The b2b trust mandate* [online]. Forrester. Available at: https://www.forrester.com/report/the-b2b-trust-mandate/res176516?objectid=res176516.

3. Caplow, B. (2021). *Three seismic shifts in buying behavior from Forrester's 2021 b2b buying study* [online]. Forrester. Available at: https://www.forrester.com/blogs/three-seismic-shifts-in-buying-behavior-from-forresters-2021-b2b-buying-survey/.

Chapter 4

1. Petrone, P. (2022). *Want higher InMail acceptance rates? Here's the best data for reaching out* [online]. LinkedIn. Available at: https://www.linkedin.com/business/sales/blog/prospecting/data-on-sending-inmails-higher-acceptance-rates.

2. Intal, C. and Lee, E. (2021). *What virtual selling actions contribute to exceeding sales targets?* [online]. LinkedIn. Available at: https://www.linkedin.com/business/sales/blog/strategy/virtual-selling-actions-assured-to-help-you-exceed-sales-targets.

3. LinkedIn Sales Solutions. (2022). *LinkedIn state of sales report 200* [online]. LinkedIn. Available at: https://www.linkedin.com/business/sales/blog/strategy/virtual-selling-actions-assured-to-help-you-exceed-sales-targets.

4. LinkedIn Sales Solutions. (2020). *Win when buyers win* [online]. Available at: https://business.linkedin.com/sales-solutions/buyer-first.

5. Havas Group. (n.d.). *Entering the age of cynicism* [online]. Available at: https://www.meaningful-brands.com/?utm_source=morning_brew.

6. Khandelwal, S., Deming, D., Hjortegaard, J.F., and Cruse, W. (2021). *Virtual selling has become simply selling* [online]. Bain & Company. Available at: https://www.bain.com/insights/virtual-selling-has-become-simply-selling/.

7. Lister, J. (2021). *The LinkedIn state of sales report 2021* [online]. LinkedIn. Available at: https://www.linkedin.com/business/sales/blog/trends/the-linkedin-state-of-sales-report-2021.

Chapter 5

1. Petrone, P. (2022). *Want higher InMail acceptance rates? Here's the best data for reaching out* [online]. LinkedIn. Available at: https://www.linkedin.com/business/sales/blog/prospecting/data-on-sending-inmails-higher-acceptance-rates.

Chapter 6

1. Eck, A. (2014). *For more effective studying, take notes with pen and paper* [online]. Pbs.org. Available at: https://www.pbs.org/wgbh/nova/article/taking-notes-by-hand-could-improve-memory-wt/.

2. Parrotte, S. (n.d.). *Making the most out of you demo questions* [online]. Chorus. Available at: https://www.chorus.ai/blog/making-the-most-out-of-your-demo-questions.

3. Reed, D. (2019). *The ultimate guide to asking sales questions (and 29 questions you can use today)* [online]. Gong. Available at: https://www.gong.io/blog/sales-questions/.

Chapter 7

1. Petrone, P. (2022). *Want higher InMail acceptance rates? Here's the best data for reaching out* [online]. LinkedIn. Available at: https://www.linkedin.com/business/sales/blog/prospecting/data-on-sending-inmails-higher-acceptance-rates.

Chapter 9

1. Shea, M. (2021). *2022 predictions: Battle-tested B2B leaders lean into their new reality* [online]. Outreach. Available at: https://www.outreach.io/resources/blog/b2b-leaders-2022-predictions.
2. Sherrard, S., Dave, R., and MacGregor, M. P. (2022). What B2Bs need to know about their buyers. *Harvard Business Review*.

Chapter 10

1. Gartner. (n.d.). *Gartner survey finds that majority of technology purchases come with high degree of regret* [online]. Available at: https://www.gartner.com/en/newsroom/press-releases/2022-07-12-gartner-finds-that-majority-of-technology-purchases-come-with-high-degree-of-regret [Accessed 6 May 2023].
2. Adamson, B. and Toman, N. (2020). *5 ways the future of b2b buying will rewrite the rules of effective selling* [online]. Gartner. Available at: https://www.gartner.com/en/documents/3988440.

Chapter 11

1. LinkedIn Sales Solutions. (2022). *LinkedIn state of sales report* 200 [online]. LinkedIn. Available at: https://www.linkedin.com/business/sales/blog/strategy/virtual-selling-actions-assured-to-help-you-exceed-sales-targets.
2. Sherrard, S., Dave, R., and MacGregor, M. P. (2022). What B2Bs need to know about their buyers. *Harvard Business Review*.

Chapter 13

1. Kurtuy, A., (2022). *60+ career change statistics for 2022 [That you didn't know!]* [online]. Novorésumé. Available at: https://novoresume.com/career-blog/career-change-statistics.

Chapter 14

1. Hyken, S. (2020). Ninety-six percent of customers will leave you for bad customer service. *Forbes*.
2. Gallo, A. (2014.) The value of keeping the right customers. *Harvard Business Review*.
3. Luck, I. (2023). 10 B2B customer retention strategies. *Customer Gauge*.
4. Keitt, T. J. (2020). Build the case for a customer success management program now. *Forrester*.
5. Thompson, E. (n.d.). Realizing the Benefits of Superior Customer Experience: A Gartner Trend Insight Report. [online] Available at: https://www.gartner.com/en/doc/3874972-realizing-the-benefits-of-superior-customer-experience-a-gartner-trend-insight-report.
6. Design and Branding Company. (n.d.). *Customer acquisition vs customer retention* [graphic]. Available at: https://studiodbc.com/infographics/customer-acquisition-retention [Accessed 8 May 2023].
7. Gartner. (2022). *Gartner says adaptable sales organizations must rethink their customer understanding, engagement and operating models* [Press release]. Available at: https://www.gartner.com/en/newsroom/press-releases/2022-05-17-gartner-says-adaptable-sales-organizations-must-rethink-ther-customer-understanding-engagement-and-operating-models.

Acknowledgments

Like any major project, in the writing of this book, many individuals have supported me during this process.

First and foremost, I am thankful for Cory Cotten-Potter. As my editor and task master, he has kept me and this project on track and assisted me throughout the process. He has poured himself into the text and takes my ideas, concepts, and strategies and creates stories and prose. I am grateful that he is on my team.

Also, I would like to thank the marketing team around this endeavor: Carolyn Monaco, Veronica Kido, Maria Doyle, Brianna Dai, and Kym Yancey. Their ideas and brilliance astound me.

I stand in awe of Todd Caponi, a client and colleague who graciously provided the Foreword to this book. Thank you.

To my coaches, Dale Robinette and Sandra Yancey: You hold me accountable and help me identify my own blind spots in leadership and execution.

The leadership team at ValueSelling Associates who makes it happen every day. You are dedicated, smart, savvy, and our organization is better for your involvement. Chris Merullo, our amazing operations guru who makes sure that all the trains run on time is my right hand. The brilliant Lorin Yeater, who can take any idea and make it look beautiful—her creative and design thinking is simply wonderful. I have never heard Lorin say, "No," regardless of the initiative or timeline. And Julie Bregen, whose process approach to growth is allowing us to scale, and who challenges me every day and makes us all better in the process.

The Wiley team has been invaluable throughout this process: Zach Schisgal, Jozette Moses, and Julie Kerr. Your guidance, patience, and leadership throughout this process has been instrumental—you are consummate professionals, and it is a pleasure to be your partner.

To my husband, Steve, for his unwavering support. You are the wind beneath my wings, and I am thankful every day that we are on this life journey today. My children, Melissa and Sam, "sell" me on their ideas and goals every day. I love you all, and you make everything I do better.

To the professionals and associates at ValueSelling Associates. Day in and day out, you make it happen for our clients. You bring ValueSelling to life and put it into practice. I stand in awe of your work ethic, your leadership, and am beyond thankful that you have chosen to share your time and talent with us at ValueSelling Associates, Inc. Thank you, Yuichi Abe, Scott Anschuetz, Su Askew, Gerard Baglieri, Franck Bichot, Greg Brown, Laurie Brown, Denise Brunton, JB Bush, Ashley Campbell, Kate Cook, Tony Cascio, Nalliby Haddad Cela, Ellen Cleary, Dawson Cochran, Frans Coenen, Rishi Dhawan, Alessandro Faorlin, Mitch Friedman, Bryan Gregory, Dominique Hans, Rob Harnett, Oliver Holroyd, Nicole Hutzul, Marilyn Janas, Dave Kahl, Theodoros Karipidis, George Kavanagh, Jens Winther, Josh Magee, Dimitris Mavromatis, Rick McAninch, Jason McKarge, Tom Miller, PJ Nisbet, Carlos Nouche, Candice October, Wolfgang Otto, Riccardo Pavanato, Peter Philpott, Natalie R. Pitchford, Gene Raphaelian, Tricia Raphaelian, Scott Reynolds, Jim Roche, Liz Roche, Chad Sanderson, Haruhisa Sato, Lisa Schnare, Mike Sowerbutts, Kevin Sun, Jon Tirpak, Bart van Eijck, Johan van Veen, Doug Von Koenig, John Weber, and Alex Zabala.

Lastly, and certainly not least, to our clients: You put your trust in us every day. You have invited us into your board rooms and your sales meetings, allowing us to partner with you to realize incredible results and outcomes. You are the reason we exist. You provide us the opportunity to do what we love with people we admire.

I have been blessed with many mentors throughout my life. Lloyd Sappington, the founder of ValueSelling Associates, is one of those pivotal people who changed my life forever.

If I have forgotten to mention anyone, it is certainly not intentional. I am fortunate to have a large group of supporters: friends, family, and colleagues who have encouraged me, helped me, challenged me, and influenced my thinking throughout this process.

Thank you, the reader, for proving that selling value is *not* a trend, but the only way forward for successful revenue professionals.

–Julie Thomas

About the Author

Julie Thomas works with revenue leaders across industries to help them realize sales results they never thought possible.

Julie is laser-focused about guiding revenue organizations through uncertainty and helping them build resilient, engaged teams that drive predictable, sustainable results—creating customers for life.

As chief executive officer and president of ValueSelling Associates, Inc., Julie leads the company's global expansion. She is responsible for its position as the market leader in on-demand, instructor-led, virtual, and hybrid (blended) learning solutions delivered in more than 17 languages.

In a career spanning 36 years, Julie credits her mastery of the ValueSelling Framework for her own meteoric rise through the ranks of sales, sales management, and corporate leadership positions.

Julie began her sales career at Gartner Group (now Gartner, Inc.). In 1999, she became vice president of Gartner's sales training for the Americas. Her role included onboarding new sales hires and driving adoption of the ValueSelling Framework. She has extensive experience applying, coaching, and reinforcing the ValueSelling Framework, Vortex Prospecting, ValueSelling Account Planning, and ValueSelling Essentials® and their application to all customer-facing roles across the revenue engine.

In 2003, Julie joined ValueSelling Associates as chief executive officer and president. She led the company to its industry leader status in competency- and process-based training for escalating sales performance in B2B sales organizations worldwide. Under Julie's leadership, ValueSelling Associates is consistently honored as an award-winning sales training service provider by a number of organizations.

In addition to her role at ValueSelling Associates, Julie is a noted speaker, consultant, and author of *ValueSelling: Driving Sales Up One Conversation at a Time*. She is a contributor to Forbes.com, the Forbes Business Development Council, and the LinkedIn Sales Blog.

Julie serves on the advisory board of the eWomenNetwork Foundation Advisory Council. She is also involved in a number of charities in the San Diego region. **Julie.Thomas@Value Selling.com**

Index

BRING **VALUE SELLING** TO YOUR COMPANY

C R E A T E :

⊕ **More predictable, sustainable results**

⤙ **More resilient, engaged teams**

🏆 **Customers for life**

Author, speaker, and CEO Julie Thomas has helped tens of thousands deliver remarkable sales results —regardless of market conditions.

Whether you want to escalate your performance, fire up your team, or level-up your onboarding, Julie and her team are ready with the power of the award-winning ValueSelling Framework® methodology, training, and toolset.

──────── **T R U S T E D B Y :** ────────

 dun&bradstreet   /LiveRamp   alteryx

🜨 TANIUM.    ✷ Kimberly-Clark
PROFESSIONAL

Contact: **PowerofValueSelling@valueselling.com** today.